EPIC ESSAYS
IN 30 MINUTES

EPIC ESSAYS
IN 30 MINUTES

Easy Tips for Writing A⁺ Essays,
7th-12th Grade Levels

Diane Stafford & Melissa Mead

Credit Line
Excerpts from THE OUTSIDERS by S.E. Hinton, copyright © 1967, renewed 1995 by S.E. Hinton. Used by permission of Viking Children's Books, an imprint of Penguin Young Readers Group, a division of Penguin Random House LLC. All rights reserved.

Graphic design and cover by Cita Graber
Cover photograph by Dylan Rigdon
ISBN: 9798764812434
Independently published.
Printed in the United States of America.

Other books by Diane Stafford
The Vitamin D Cure (coauthor Jim Dowd, M.D.)
Migraines for Dummies (coauthor Jennifer Shoquist, M.D.)
No More Panic Attacks (coauthor Jennifer Shoquist, M.D.)
1000 Best Job-Hunting Secrets (coauthor Moritza Day)
The New Low-Carb Way of Life (coauthor Rob Thompson, M.D.)
Potty Training for Dummies (coauthor Jennifer Shoquist, M.D.)
60,001 Best Baby Names
Parenting Guide (several authors)
The Ultimate Baby Names Book
50,001 Best Baby Names
The Big Book of 60,00 Baby Names
Syndrome W (coauthor Harriette Mogul, M.D.)
40,001 Best Baby Names

Dedication

To *young writers* we know and love: London, Ben, Romano, Isabella, Joey, Liliana, Eamon, Joaquin, Amanda, Mateo, Josie, Ella, Samantha, Liam, Ethan, Patrick, Matthew, and Luke.

To *incredible teachers:* For your intelligence, hard work, dedication, and patience, you deserve love, support, and appreciation every day of the week.

To teens: Believe in yourself, and ignore that little voice that warns "don't write what you *really* think or you'll be judged." You have the right to voice your own one-of-a-kind thoughts.

Here's your hard 'ask' as a writer: Invite your readers to consider the arguments you advance in essays. Your freshly minted ideas matter. Thus, you should take pride in presenting them in essays. Every single day, enjoy the freedom of expressing yourself.

No one has ever seen the world exactly the way you do. Your words resonate. You are relevant. Polish your essays, and people will love reading what you have to say. That's why we wrote this book for you!

Foreword: Epic Essays

Eons ago, pre-COVID, you had your life cosmically aligned—or so it seemed. Then came the pandemic and Distance Learning, with chips and dips, puppy-dog-covered sleep pants, and tons of loose ends. Zoom learning days made you grow fearful of The Big, Bad Classroom even though you *knew* you would have to return there eventually. Nevertheless, you dreaded that day because surely people would be staring at you and wondering why you seemed so clueless, your knowledge apparently all gone.

Fortunately, though, the reality has been better than expected, right? Even though you have to wear a mask, seeing friends and teachers is comforting, and getting out of the house isn't half bad. Overall, you're surprised that the transition has been seamless—that is, until the day your English teacher assigned that first essay, which unhinged you just like it did pre-pandemic. Hair-pulling and pencil-throwing accompanied the war cry "I have nothing to write!" Your parents groaned. You wept. It reminded you all over again how much you had hated writing essays, and now things were worse because you had lost your confidence, swept away in Zoom dust.

Would a cookie help? Or a tutor whispering ideas

in your ear? The fact is, just frame the situation right, and you'll revel in being *alive and in person*, easily shrugging off Distance Learning flashbacks. There is no doubt that you can display the spectacular voice that is uniquely yours. *No one has ever seen the world the way you do, and that is what your authorial voice will showcase.* Furthermore, you have supportive people (family and teachers) waiting-hoping-yearning to read what you write when you put pen to paper and fingers to keys.

You're going to write with a secret tingling in your heart—a sense that you're perfectly equipped for this essay path because your mind now teems with fresh ideas from living-the-teen-life and from reading *Epic Essays in 30 Minutes*. While you used to waste your mad genius on texting, now you're swooping up that individuality and putting it to work for you. Go ahead. Show off. Share your zingy words with your teachers, your class, your world—and people will discover how fascinating you are.

Think of it. Today you actually are a wiser and wilier kid than you were pre-COVID. It does not matter that the essay-writing skills you had back in your "other life" have gone the way of half-nibbled red crayons, and in their place are Zoom talents of dodging and hunkering down, out of sight. You learned how to study while masked and mute, hiding behind the cloak of dark Zoom screens and sometimes not uttering a single word.

Why is this a good thing? In reality, you *grew*. It was survival of the fittest, and you came out of it a sturdy and resilient Zoom veteran. That makes you more textured, more complex—frankly, a specimen of humanity that scientists would love to study just to find out how forced isolation affects young people.

In the virtual environment, you lost instant access to teachers, those almost omniscient human beings who formerly kept you on track. Schedules. End games. Gold stars. Yes, sadly, teacher/student bonds frayed, leaving kids untethered, roaming around in space like astronauts on a moonwalk. Even high achievers began to see teachers as faraway heavenly specters or holograms. Truly, you hated the uncertainty of it all, especially being unable to nail down anything academically.

On the up side, though, you emerged a champion daydreamer, with prize nuggets floating in your head. This puts you in great position to capitalize on those ideas and put them to work in exceptional essays. As a more mature and actualized teen than before the pandemic, you are now ready to speak out and be heard. Thankfully, you have teachers at your side to motivate you, lead you, and instruct you.

In truth, slacking wasn't as much fun as you thought when Zoom learning first started, and now you are *learning* in a real-life school environment. All of us saw the reasons that summer break doesn't last forever. Most of us can handle just so much of loud music, low hygiene standards, and crummy clothes.

At any rate, today's newly chic students are looking for great outcomes:

- You want essay writing to feel "lighter."
- You produce *better* material without a skeleton frame or organizer.
- You thrive on feedback and praise.

Furthermore, you'll be happy that *Epic Essays in 30 Minutes* shows you how to take an essay from start to finish, providing examples, and ending with here's-what-I-was-trying-to-say. This easy process allows you to write an essay that says exactly what you intended. Suddenly, your work is elevated to the stack of "best essays in class." Can that coveted A+ be far behind?

Tools in Your Trunk

So, slick back your Epic-Essay mullet and get ready for a fun ride. We fully understand that a Generation Z kid like you has no patience for snail-slow, pre-Internet days because you were born with an iPad in your hand, and a week later you were teething on your mother's cell phone. Essentially, electronics have reset you into a short-attention-span, glory-seeking honey badger. Generally speaking, you don't care what happens as long as you can swipe, text, post, and marvel at the globe-trotting, wealth-accruing lives that people create online. You are hooked; you can barely move without a cell phone.

Obviously, living an Internet-tinged existence does require different school tools from the ones your parents had growing up. Fortunately, *Epic Essays in 30 Minutes* is here to hand you a smooth ride. Absorb. Breathe. Take the keys we hand you, and adopt an in-class attitude that screams positivity. In days, you'll be saying, "I've got this."

Shifting Gears

Of course, stacking up ideas for essays is not fast. To your haste-driven mind, it even sounds *complicated*. However, you can get used to switching from "drive" to "park," as quality writing rises in importance on your list of priorities. If you hate the moment when a teacher asks you to move from the flash-bang notification-gaming amusement park into the quiet sanctuary of essay writing, think of this Zen unwinding as the perfect chance to free your writer's voice. Share your thoughts right after you draw on those stunning ideas dashing around in your brain.

Get chummy with this book's user-friendly method that makes your essay-writing days feel cool and expressive, not cumbersome or difficult. Your mind selects thoughts. You magically use our four

Gs—GRAB, GAB, GOODBYE, GLUE—for a quick prewrite in which you write or type your thoughts. Then sit back and let the essay grow "cold" overnight. Finally, you review what you wrote and delete weak or weird parts. *Voila!* You wind up with a final essay that is a super-slick work of art. Proudly, you turn it in or hit "submit" online.

You will enjoy speaking out because you have *lots* on your mind. For this interesting quest, enlist supporters—older siblings, parents, teachers—the more praise, the better! On the road to Epic Essay success, take a few people along for the ride, and ask them to give you kudos anytime the notion hits them. Your fresh thoughts will be people-pleasers, and someone is bound to notice that you are awesome.

If You Feel Antsy in a Classroom…

On days when you still feel restless in the classroom, remind yourself that you have two huge assets: *cyber genius and plucky courage.* Those got you through the pandemic, and they now serve as a springboard for becoming a superstar essay writer. Fear nothing. Expect everything. Exude optimism. With new knowledge and deep thoughts, you can save the day for the English language as we know it and keep the beautiful written word from declining into a junkyard of Tweets and emojis.

In the process of hitching your wagon to essay stars, you'll say goodbye to check sheets and organizers. No more taking apart essays and trying to put them back together into a readable piece of writing. Designed especially for grid kids facing this New Day of Education, our **Autopilot Essay** is a nitty-gritty fast-write that is easy to master. Then, for a bigger challenge, tackle the more sophisticated **Cruise-Control Essay.** This model inspires phenomenal writing and offers insights into terms you'll need for AP tests, the SAT, and the ACT.

At any rate, having *Epic Essays in 30 Minutes* in the house means your parents can breathe again, and you can *enjoy* writing, perhaps for the first time ever. That's why we happily rebrand essay writing as a "hot new hobby" for this era. We make essay skills accessible and finesse the road trip so that excelling as a writer becomes whip-smart cool and not hard at all.

Essays make you think. Essays make you write. Essays make you deliver. These are three key life skills. Plus, Autopilot Essay writing *always* ends with you feeling in charge of your "grade fate," and that can be a welcome feeling.

Although many Electronics Age kids have a learning curve when it comes to drilling down on a single topic, *you* can vow to work on focus. Just accept the fact that you get restless after spending hours tapping, texting, electro-talking, and phone-checking, and that's why you get impatient when a parent or teacher tries to interrupt and communicate with you. In your mind, a timer clicks and says, "Please, *for the love of God*, hurry up." What you learn from this reaction is that you *must* develop patience.

Set aside specific times for electronics. You can't let these excellent, exciting modes of communication ruin healthy relationships. Listening matters, and that means you must have an ear for parents, teachers, and anyone else who deserves full attention—even kids that your teacher teams you with for "group work."

Epic Essays in 30 Minutes preps you to write capably *and* keep up with tomorrow's world of 2050—a future when you will be reinventing yourself over and over. In the short run and the long run, you'll be thrilled to learn how to write an Autopilot Essay because you'll no longer be that slowpoke forced to the gravel shoulder of the road. Try this nice, smooth essay ride facilitated by the remarkable ability to park your words in *just the right places*.

So, Why Write Essays?

Here are a few of many reasons you'll want to develop good writing skills:

- You will fill out job applications someday.
- You will write college admissions essays that clinch college acceptances.

- You will write in the business world and present yourself as a literate individual who is ready to contribute to corporate projects.
- You will want to express yourself well in personal correspondences.
- You will be thankful when you no longer struggle for words.
- You must become a competent writer to be effective as an articulate citizen of the world.
- You will want to write a love note to someone you cherish.

Bottom line, you're way too smart to let bad habits mess with your mind. You don't want to be 100% defined as a gamer, texter, Instagram star, or posting person. When it's time to essay-write, ignore electronics, and let thoughts flow naturally. Reading, learning, and gravitating toward greatness are your new marching orders as a competent young writer.

Hey, you're at school, anyway, so why not just write A+ essays while you're there?

CONTENTS

Foreword

PART I:
The Autopilot Essay

Get your motor revved! You're going to unearth epic writing in any spot where you can snuggle down and do some super-deep thinking. You will suffer no more of that "I don't know what to write" agony because your words will pop into place like wildflowers on a roadside. *Seize the day.* You're going to have fun being a standard-bearer for the A Team.

Chapter One:
Go to Word-Stock

Tip for the Day: Anxious. Angst. Angry. If you're feeling any of these "A" emotions, that just means you're normal. In your class of 25, probably 23 feel the same way. Take comfort. You will get reenergized. Give yourself time.

Here's your prep for turning out Epic Essays. Think of this book like Woodstock on steroids. You've seen photos from the days when "Flower Children" of the '60s danced and sang in an era that looked somewhat magical. In truth, Woodstock was more like decadence and unwashed bodies although groundbreaking music did endure. Most memorable, though, was the event's youthful spirit of self-revelation; that was a keeper.

Indeed, ideas bloomed August 15-18, 1969, at Woodstock, held at a 600-acre dairy farm, in Bethel, New York, and maybe your own great-grandparents were among those bell-bottomed hippies writing poetry and rhapsodizing with flowers in their hair. Although cursed by rain, bad drug "trips," and equipment glitches, the festival went down in history as a landmark moment in rock 'n' roll (Peacock).

Flash forward. Now, we want you to imagine a songfest today. What song would you write for Gen Z's "pretend" festival? Get some dreaminess going on and jot down thoughts that come to mind as you conjure up a vision of your peers singing songs, reading poetry, and just loving being young…on the lawn, in the rain, in your town.

Let's call your event "Word-Stock," and this becomes your go-to mental and physical space for writing. Every day, write or read. Choose the place, the topic, the length—even the type of text. Experiment: Write a short story. A poem. A news article. A song. Or just a few lines of nothing in particular. Then, the next day, repeat.

Channel words and thoughts. Sit cross-legged or at a table or desk—and write your little heart out, alone or with others. Allow your brain some slow-

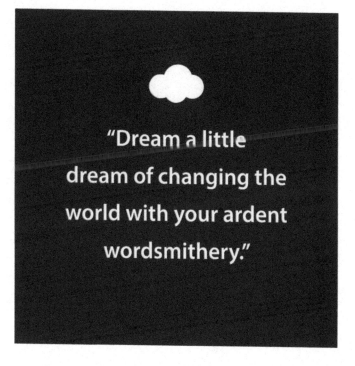

"Dream a little dream of changing the world with your ardent wordsmithery."

paced time to become enchanted with the idea of seizing the truth of your thoughts on paper, in your head, or in your computer. Dream a little dream of changing the world with your ardent wordsmithery.

The goal? Seek the absolute wonderment you had as a child when your parents first read *Goodnight Moon* to you. Here's the plan.

The Scene:

- Find a super-comfortable place to write.
- For skull safety during the upcoming tsunami

of exploding ideas, wear a baseball cap, hat,
tiara, or flower wreath.

- Use music (or snacks) to establish a mood of
your choosing.
- Write on a topic you care about.
- Use computer, notebook paper, or writing
pads.
- Make your writing as long or short as you
want.
- Think of readers you value and write for
them.
- Have a specific purpose for writing *each day*.
- Craft interesting sentences.

The Point:

Write in a way that engages readers. Enjoy
playing with words, moving them around to see how
it changes sentences. If you want a teacher's or
parent's take on your writing, request an
instructor/learner session and listen to their
observations. The point is to enrich the "language"
person in you with daily writes.

The Publish:

Publish for your audience—an Internet blog or
email to your grandmother or a letter to the editor of
your school paper or a close friend. When you finish
reading a book, post comments about it on the *Epic
Essays in 30 Minutes* blog that is just waiting to hear

from you (see dianestafford.org). Or just share thoughts with one of your contacts. Also, post your comments on what other people have said about books they have read.

Rules of the Road for Posts:

1. Write positives, not negatives. Don't critique authors or other people who post.
2. Instead of saying a book is "really good," say what's good about it—the characters are realistic, the tone is frightening, it helped you go to sleep, etc.
3. Do not pontificate (if you don't know what "pontificate" means, check Webster's Dictionary online). ALWAYS look up words you don't know.
4. Do not use all-caps in posts.
5. Stick to the formal language you use in essays. Remember, you are a writer who is writing *what you think* about a book.

In the end, make your trip to Word-Stock count. Don't take detours that waste time, and enjoy the ease of achieving essay stardom. Remember, every day of your life, you're the hero of your own epic journey, and that calls for writing that is uplifting as well as hard-hitting, focused as well as sensational.

Chapter Two:
Promise and Deliver

Tip for the Day: You are exactly where you belong—at this school with these teachers and with these classmates.

Writing a formal essay calls for getting out of the starting blocks by letting your readers know what you want to tell them—a capsule version. Make a promise. Say something like this: Readers will learn why freshmen in high school need older 'buddies' to mentor them. OR: Having a dad who is a pro basketball player is not an automatic advantage. OR: Becoming a ballet dancer is not as simple as buying toe shoes and taking lessons.

The first few sentences of an essay tell the reader where you are going. In other words, the unsaid promise or thesis sentence (also called a topic sentence) sums up your entire essay. Place it anywhere in the introductory paragraph—beginning, middle, or end—but be sure you include it as a key road direction for your essays. It's as important as the green "Go" on stoplights.

When you text, you don't leave the juicy part till the end, do you? Instead, you start with the "big headline" that tells a friend where you're headed. **Example: GUESS WHO I SAT BY AT LUNCH TODAY?** (Grammatically speaking, though, it should be "whom.") Anyway, make your essay *as intriguing as an enthusiastic text.* (Of course, writing formal essays means using third person, with words like "it," "he," "she," "they," and "the reader" or "readers." Avoid "I," "me," "we," and "you.")

Know where you're going. Act like you're hiking in unknown woods, and before you leave, you tell your mom or dad where you're going. You need a destination plan: *Taking a long hike through Back Bay Park, a walker starts at the Orientation Building and proceeds until the trail ends at the sidewalk outside the Dover Shores neighborhood.*

Your topic sentence promises readers they will learn about something specific. Experiment with these topics: high-school buddy system, basketball heritage, or ballet success. *Example: Each freshman starting high school needs an older "buddy" for guidance along the path of a new learning and geographical experience.* Then explain three advantages that a buddy provides: understanding the campus map, getting off to a good start with teachers, and asking a counselor for schedule changes. Easy.

Note that in the following paragraph, the topic sentence is the SECOND sentence rather than the first. This is okay, too. The writer describes a high school freshman's state of mind. Next, in the topic sentence, the Space Station idea continues when the writer mentions "universe."

Example: Starting high school is a little bit like going on the International Space Station because a freshman feels insecure, lost, and nervous. However, in this new universe, an upper-class "buddy" comes to the rescue with a campus map, counselor information, and teacher tips.

Write in present tense. Above, we used the verbs "is," "feels," "comes." Instead of using past tense "was," "felt," and "came," you are writing in the here and now, and that is the case for most formal essays.

Also, avoid contractions. Glance back over your writing and change "don't" to "do not" and "isn't" to "is not" and so on. Easy-peasy! Look for the apostrophe as a reminder. However, leave in place apostrophes that indicate possession, such as "A

11

freshman's job the first day is complicated." That kind of apostrophe *stays*. You get rid of contractions.

Examine the following topic sentence, and think: *How would I get rid of contractions?* Also, how would you change the sentence from past to present tense?

According to research, about two-thirds of track and field athletes competing at the U.S. Olympic Trials in Eugene, Oregon, over the past two weeks were regular caffeine consumers, and they didn't have to change this habit.

Corrected:

According to research, about two-thirds of track and field athletes competing at the U.S. Olympic Trials in Eugene, Oregon, over the past two weeks **are** regular caffeine consumers, but there **is** no reason to change this habit.

When essay writing, toss out ***past tense*** and **contractions.** Stick this "notation" in your mind and keep it there. If you see an example of past tense in your writing that you don't know how to correct, ask your teacher to show you. The sooner you get good at this, the better. In two days, it will be like starting your engine—a no-brainer.

Example: Let's say your teacher asks you to write about O. Henry's short story "The Gift of the Magi," and you start with this first sentence: *He has no idea what his wife got him for Christmas, and she has no idea what her husband got her, but both want to choose gifts that reflect the great love they share* (Henry).

This topic sentence is a "GRAB." You are hinting, "Hey, I know you're busy, but please read what I wrote, and you'll be glad you did." The reader wonders "hmmm, what will this couple give each other for Christmas?"

TAG, You're It!

Often, your topic sentence refers to a book, play, poem, short story, or other text that you're reading in class. In that case, you must include the "TAG" thing you learned in sixth grade. This information informs as to what text you studied for this essay. *Example:* In the nonfiction book *The Year of Magical Thinking,* written by Joan Didion, readers learn about mourning from a masterful writer known for clarity and candor.

Then, include examples from the book that illustrate how Didion's messages on handling grief have great impact. TAG works like this:

- Title: *The Year of Magical Thinking*
- Author: Joan Didion
- Genre: Nonfiction book

Furthermore, TAG doesn't have to follow that "TAG" order. Notice how in the following example, the arrangement is: Genre, Title, Author. Sometimes, the TAG reads more effectively in a different sequence. *Example*: In the tragedy *Macbeth,* written by English playwright William Shakespeare, three witches set off a chain of deaths when they inform Macbeth that he is going to be king of Scotland; he kills the current ruler, a few more people, and soon there is a civil war.

TAG information belongs in a topic sentence. This nuts-and-bolts part tells your reader *what you read, who wrote it,* and *what kind of literature it is* (novel, nonfiction book, poem, short story, editorial, article).

T: Title (what you read)

A: Author (who wrote it)

G: Genre (what kind of text it is)

You know what a title is. You know what an author is. But do you know what "genre" is? Genre, pronounced "zhaan-ruh," refers to a group designation for a work of writing, also known as a text. Is your class reading a short story? A poem? A novel? A play? A poem? When you identify what you read, you refer to a work of fiction as a novel, short story, poem, play, or fantasy. Works of fiction are not true stories; these feature imaginary events and people. If you read nonfiction, you identify it as an article, biography, history, textbook, essay, or nonfiction book. Works of nonfiction are based on facts, truths, and real people. Nonfiction works instruct, inform, persuade, or entertain.

The following topic sentences have TAGs in place:

In the student essay "Defining a Home," by Sammy Smith, readers learn that a home is always more than a built structure with walls and a foundation.

The short story "The Tell-Tale Heart," by Edgar Allan Poe, has a haunting tone that makes readers uneasy but too curious to stop reading (Poe).

Get Used to 'Adulting'

Often, your first impulse when asked to write a paragraph is to use the kinds of topic sentences you wrote in sixth grade for personal narratives. You know the ones. Instead of starting a Spring Break essay with an exciting happening or a flashy sights-and-sounds description, you say, "Here is what I did on Spring Break…" or you might say, "This is how I spent my time in Florida…" Or "Something I like to do on Spring Break is…"

But *no, no, and no.* These are fine when you're a little kid—perfect, actually. Now, though, you're a teen writing formal essays. Therefore, you're no longer going to use "I" or "my" or "me" or "we" in a formal essay. You've been there. You've done that. In fact, though, "I" and "my" and "me" and "we" belong primarily in personal narratives and memoirs.

15

The formal essay, on the other hand, requires "he/she/they/it" and "the reader" or "readers" or "one." (Save the conversational "you" and "we" for chatty column writing or personal communications or a book like the one in your hand.)

The GRAB is the topic sentence. This is your way of snagging a reader's attention. *Example:* Snakes come in many varieties, but all have an eerie and ominous reputation.

Or you can choose a fancier "GRAB." *Examples:*

- *Ask a question.* Did you know Generation Z writes more than any generation ever?

- *Use a comparison.* Some people say that cats are the aloof members of the pet world because unlike dogs, they are not known for being "cuddlers."

- *State an interesting fact.* Although many teens claim to be great multitaskers, researchers argue that no one actually does several things simultaneously without sacrificing quality.

- *Set the scene with a description.* "Dark and ominous, the winding path leads to a house that neighborhood kids love to explore for its scary atmosphere of whistling winds and unexplained noises." Instantly, the essay becomes a page-turner because you want to know what is happening.

- *Shock or excite.* Honeybees should line up for "Dancing with the Stars." The worker bees dance in the direction of flowers so that they and fellow bees have a spot for drawing nectar.

Become a Persuader

Write an introduction that gets readers' attention. Then decide what you want to include in the three body paragraphs that come next. For each, present a reason why your readers should agree with your

"Using a great global statement as a hook to draw in readers is an excellent way to start an essay."

perspective on the topic. The first sentence of each paragraph should argue for your side. Follow up that topic sentence with a quote, fact, or an example that underscores the argument you are conveying in that paragraph. Then go into more detail about the evidence that backs up your topic sentence and overall argument.

Sample different methods of persuasion. State facts and statistics. Relate an anecdote (story). Share expert opinions. Describe experiences. Decide what you think works best to win over your readers. Also, end each body paragraph with a summary sentence that explains what that paragraph set out to prove and also harks back to your original thesis.

Using a great global statement as a hook to draw in readers is an excellent way to start an essay. From there, power forward by writing strong paragraphs that stay on the topic and present reasons, arguments, or points—boom, boom, boom, one, two, three. Then the only thing you have left to do is wrap up what you were arguing or explaining and use words that leave readers satisfied and maybe even impressed.

Roll It Out

A simple setup for an essay goes like this:

Introduction (GRAB):

- Hooks the reader's attention with catchy

words.

- Has a topic sentence "promise" that tells what the essay will prove or explain.

Essay Body (GAB):

- Mentions points that support the topic sentence.
- For each point, you start a new paragraph.
- Starts with a topic sentence that shows where each paragraph is headed.
- Includes evidence quotes (GAB) from the text that you read in class.
- Has a paragraph wrap-up in the last sentence.

Conclusion (GOODBYE):

- Sums up the essay.
- Repeats the message of the topic sentence in different words.
- Adds no brand-new information.

Throughout your essay, apply GLUE (transition words) to ensure that your sentences don't sound too chop-chop-choppy.

What's Up in the Classroom?

In junior high (middle school) and high school, you'll do several types of writing:

- **Expository:** This is an informative essay

that explains a topic or idea.

- **Persuasive:** This kind of essay argues a certain viewpoint.

- **Literature-based essay:** A student writer analyzes one aspect of a literary work (poem, short story, novel, etc.).

- **Research paper:** A long, research-based essay explores a research question; the paper includes in-text citations and a Works Cited (bibliography) at the end.

After you finish your classroom days, someday in the working world, you will write reports, emails, business letters, ads, presentations, proposals, and project assessments.

Chapter Three:
Write Great Global Statements

Tip for the Day: No more falling back on the crutch of your war wounds from Distance Learning. Was it difficult during the pandemic to hone writing skills and maintain focus in your Zoom classes? Sure, it was! (I taught via DL, and I promise you that it was difficult for instructors to keep your attention.) However, there are always ways to excel, regardless of learning mode. Onward, upward, forward.

Global statements are not "musts" for essays. However, they do add pizzazz. Don't underestimate their impact. You have already been practicing writing topic sentences for different prompts. So, while you're at it, invest some time in what you might want to plant right before the topic sentence, which is a "global statement."

In essence, this is a catchy line that serves as a statement of purpose and attracts the attention of the reader. You can use an old saying or adage, a famous person's quote, a bulletproof piece of data, or an earth-shattering statistic. Incidentally, these are called "global" because they express a sentiment that is not just applicable to your one essay but *an overall truth for all of mankind.* Whether in Swahili, French, or English, the idea is the same.

Here's how it works. Assume you have chosen the prompt *"There is more to a person than meets the eye."* Of course, your argument will be that every single person has fascinating potential. That said, what would be a striking statement that applies globally? You might choose one of these as a global statement:

- "Each person has his strong point." Aesop (c. 620-560 BC).
- "Do not judge a book by its cover." American proverb.
- "Being different is good; embrace it." Simon Cowell ("Top Thirty Quotes of Simon Cowell").

While global statements are optional, after you get your writer's engine warmed up, these will come

"Most writers put the thesis sentence at the end of the introductory paragraph."

to mind all the time. Even posting on social media, you may want to throw in a global statement now and then. Catch people off guard and increase your audience. What often gives essays "zing" is a grab-them-by-the-neck opening sentence. Write something catchy, fun, or startling. Global statements can be assets on your quest for A+ essays.

Getting in a Pathos Groove

Here's how you can do it. Let's say you're writing

an essay in which you want to explain why the classic novel *Jane Eyre* (1847) literally defines the rhetorical appeal *pathos*— emotion-evoking. From the opening page, author Charlotte Bronte encourages readers to feel sorry for poor Jane, the outsider, which calls for a global statement establishing mood-setting gloom. She shows the girl burdened with "a heart saddened by the chidings of Bessie, the nurse, and humbled by my consciousness of physical inferiority to Eliza, John, and Georgiana Reed" (13). Jane is also excluded "from privileges intended only for contented, happy little children," to which she responds, "What does Bessie say I have done?" (13). Making matters worse, the brutal 14-year-old son of Jane's benefactress injures 10-year-old Jane, only to have the servants distort the events so drastically that Jane is locked away in the "red-room." Obviously, after these initial visceral impressions of her life as a woebegone ward languishing amid a family's "natural children," you, as a writer, stand ready to tear at readers' heartstrings.

Here is a possible global statement: *Sometimes an orphan's life is filled with dread, darkness, and doom*. Then the next sentence must move the reader's attention toward the thesis statement, setting out what the essay seeks to prove. The second sentence links the catchy first sentence with the thesis. *Second sentence: Clearly, no one can please tormenters who view her chiefly as an intruder.*

Sentence three, you will state the problem the essay will tackle—you introduce the issue: *In essence, Jane Eyre, having no supporters, family, or money, faces an uphill battle in life, and the author's appeal to pathos is wildly successful, buffeted by descriptions of so many misfortunes in so little time.*

The introduction also gives readers key background details. As an orphan in the household of her Aunt Reed at Gateshead, Jane struggles to survive spoiled children and a cruel regime at Lowood charity school until she eventually lands a governess job at Thornfield, where she finds love and hope through sheer integrity and strong spirit. Just when it seems Jane cannot get past the final impediment to marrying her beloved Mr. Rochester, she achieves a solution, which ends in self-actualization far beyond what Victorian society typically allows. *The entire process of navigating dangerous secrets, unfair treatment, and discrimination steamrolls readers into a pathos-driven orbit of enormous concern as well as heartfelt hope for poor Jane Eyre.*

This, your thesis sentence, is the last sentence of the introductory paragraph and contains the essay's topic and advances the idea you're going to argue. Notice how the verb "steamrolls" makes a strong impression. Most writers put the thesis sentence at the end of the introductory paragraph.

As for a global statement, the easiest way to write

one is to do it after you have already written the entire introduction because you know where you are going with the argument. By the way, if you like the idea of using a global statement at the start, think of a sentence that sums up the "moral of the story" or the theme or lesson, but it also must be a statement that applies to similar situations worldwide—again, that's why it's called "*global.*"

Chapter Four:
Travel the Four-G Speedway

Tip for the Day: Feeling confident? Then ask the educator at the head of the classroom if you can be a Team Leader. If you feel capable of leading the class, you can be a communicator who suggests things like breakout rooms for groups and peer tutoring for essay writing.

Understandably, that antsy brain won't leave you alone until you share some of those one-of-a-kind thoughts that are spinning around in your brain, sometimes dancing, twisting, and gyrating themselves silly. Cruising down the road, you will follow the Autopilot Essay cues GRAB, GAB, GLUE,

GOODBYE. (And, yes, you still include the informational sentence called TAG, which refers to title, author, genre.)

Now, use your brain's bright lights to focus on the next four paragraphs of this book. Why? Simple. Once you really, truly grasp the four Gs, you literally have the "keys to the car" of essay writing. Think. Absorb. Reread. Ponder. These come in handy every single time you sit down to write an essay. Commit them to memory just like you memorized your home address or phone number when you were a little kid.

GRAB: Start with a GRAB sentence that gets the attention of your reading audience. Commonly known as a topic sentence, this sets out your intentions—what you plan to deliver by writing this essay or paragraph.

GAB: Next, include "gab"—a quote from your text (book, short story, poem). For the GAB part, you will thread into place a RELEVANT quote from the book you are reading in class (or the reference text you found online). We emphasize "relevant" because you want to support the idea that you set out to prove. That means you can't choose just *any* random, willy-nilly quote. It has to relate to the topic at hand. Next, write two or three sentences that explain why you think the GAB quote supports your argument.

GLUE: Super-stick sentences together with

connecting "glue" words. See the long list of glue words in this chapter, also known as transitions or connectors; the list shows exactly the right sentence situation for each kind of glue. The trick is to make your sentences flow from one to another. That way, you don't wind up with paragraphs that sound "choppy" or list-like. For example, glue words/phrases such as "however" and "moreover" and "secondly" will make readers continue.

As you become a clever glue person, you'll discover that it's quite a spectacle, the way glue takes a few plodding sentences and links them together, like little girls holding hands as they skip down the sidewalk. It is a very cool moment because glue takes your writing from a dull list to a flowing paragraph.

GOODBYE: End the essay by wrapping up ideas in a clear conclusion. Mention one more time what you set out to prove or argue or explain and how you made your point. Then check over the paragraph you wrote to make sure you have complete sentences, ones of different lengths, and zero run-on sentences. Use about seven sentences, with the last one being your GOODBYE.

GRAB-GAB-GLUE-GOODBYE. Practice till it's second nature to use these four guys. Then you know how to write an essay. Plant the four Gs firmly in your mind. GRAB, GAB, GLUE, and GOODBYE.

Write a GRAB Topic Sentence

Below are some "facts" you can use in writing a topic sentence that tells readers what's coming (in the essay). GRAB them.

- Parents like school uniforms.

- Some kids cannot afford school uniforms.

- Many teens complain about having to wear school uniforms.

- Opinions are mixed as to whether uniforms actually make good first impressions.

- One argument against school uniforms is that these make everyone "alike," but it is also true that similar outfits cannot camouflage individuality.

We asked some students to write topic sentences. Now we want you to choose the topic sentence that is the best of the ones below.

1) People have mixed opinions on school uniforms.
2) School uniforms are boring.
3) Both beneficial and negative effects come from wearing school uniforms.
4) There are pros and cons to wearing school uniforms.
5) *Plaids. Pleated skirts. Crisp khaki pants.*

Odds are, a school uniform is the first
image that comes to mind, and this is not
always a lightweight subject.

*The best topic sentences are 1 and 5. Average ones are 3 and 4.
The worst is 2.*

Think and Write

Here's a sample paragraph that shows how to use
GRAB-GAB-GLUE-GOODBYE. (Notice the
underlined **GLUE** words and phrases.)

GRAB: Crime does not pay. The short story *The
Ransom of Red Chief*, written by O. Henry, is a tale of a
kidnapping gone bad when two men nab a kid so
annoying that they have to pay the father to take him
back.

(By the way, "crime does not pay" is a global
statement, which is "cute" but not required—kind of
like adding whipped cream to a cake. The second
sentence is *required*—it's the topic sentence, and this
one includes the important TAG.)

GAB: <u>At the start</u>, the kidnappers wonder if they
have made a mistake when one of them admits, "I
never lost my nerve yet till we kidnapped that two-
legged skyrocket of a kid" (Henry). <u>Apparently</u>, the
kidnappers decide the boy is too bratty for any father
to be willing to pay a ransom. Even the dad himself
knows his kid is unmanageable and thinks anyone

31

who would kidnap "Red Chief" has to be stupid.

GOODBYE: <u>Eventually,</u> both kidnappers get their fill of being kicked and gladly pay the father $250 to take the boy off their hands. <u>Hence</u>, this story proves "what goes around comes around." In this **GOODBYE**, two sentences wrap up the paragraph. (Note: A smart sixth-grader in Mrs. Moss's class at Mariners Elementary in Newport Beach, California, came up with the clever final sentence. Thank you, Bree! The entire class wrote global statements and chose hers as the best.)

Glue Like Crazy!

When you are gluing in transition words that hold everything together, aim for "sticky sentences." Include both "working words" and "glue words." Working words provide meaning and deliver information; glue words serve as the scaffolding and structure for a balanced, eye-catching sentence.

Add glue to sentences (see below). Make sure these transitions fit what the sentence says. Usually, you can choose from several GLUE options that will fit nicely into the sentence.

(Incidentally), there are many valid reasons for walking or riding a bike to school.

Paul is her best friend. (Therefore), she can ask for his advice.

It is a writer's job to convince a reader to take a specific action. (Thus), the writer is using persuasive skills.

Belonging is important, and it happens only when a person understands the "rules of the road" for a certain group. In a family, (therefore), each person has duties, and it is key to make sure one's own are helpful to other members of the tribe.

(Ideally), the widespread expression of thoughts on the Internet should be a positive, but in today's society, speaking out does not always improve conversations.

Life is in a constant state of change. (However), parts of lives always remain the same.

In all of the above sentences, the GLUE words *fit* the message. They help the sentences flow so that they are more readable. Without them in place, you would have choppy, unlinked sentences that leave readers cold.

Look at your own paragraph. Does it read more like a list than a paragraph that tells a story? Fix by applying "word glue." Open your bag of tricks and choose transitions that fit to glue sentences together. Sprinkle paragraphs with transitions that act as *glue*.

Here are GLUE words/phrases to open a paragraph: Consequently, therefore, thus, for example, such as, in particular, particularly, as an illustration, to illustrate, for instance, notably, especially, essentially. These words are typically adverbs, which means they "add" to the verb and modify or set the tone for a time, place.

GLUE words/phrases that cement sentences together within a paragraph: however, also, in addition, thus, essentially, basically, indeed, further, furthermore, also, in addition, too, alternatively, on the other hand, actually, as a matter of fact, besides, additionally.

GLUE words/phrases to show an effect: As a result, because (of this), as a consequence, consequently, hence, for this reason, accordingly, therefore, thus, under those circumstances, then, otherwise, in that case.

GLUE words/phrases for linking: Subsequently, eventually, previously, afterward, before (this event), next, then, anyway, at any rate, incidentally, by the way, first, second, third, secondly, thirdly, namely, for a start, initially, to start with, hence, similarly, in the first place, to begin with, initially, for a start, in that case, otherwise, if so, if not, however.

GLUE words/phrases for countering/conceding a point: either way, in either event, all the same, at any rate, conversely, from another viewpoint.

GLUE words/phrases that end an essay are:
Overall, in the end, finally, as a final point, at last, lastly, given these points, in short, therefore, hence, in summary, moreover.

Keep this list handy because it shows where different transitions fit best to enhance what the sentence says. Typically, several options work.

A Sophomore's Use of GLUE

Find the GLUE in the following excerpt from a sophomore's essay. These words and phrases unite the sentences. Also, locate the TAG (title, author, genre). By the way, all the GLUE is in boldface type.

Student Essay

Social critic/writer Henry L. Mencken conveys outspoken opinions in his 1926 satirical essay "The Penalty of Death," in which he entertains Americans with a humorous analysis of the purpose of capital punishment and its effect on society. Establishing his ethos as a patriotic citizen and an advocate for the death penalty, the author argues that capital punishment is essential simply because humans instinctively crave revenge. Through the use of satire and the invocation of pathos and logos, Mencken makes the controversial topic approachable as he seeks to convince readers that the death penalty serves as a crime deterrent.

According to the author, the failure of opposing sides to explain what this experience is like for the person being executed shows how their argument is unmethodical and hence should not be supported. **In making his case,** Mencken uses slang terms (grisly ones) for death that are cringeworthy. Mencken hopes readers will agree that it is illogical to abolish the death penalty. **Furthermore,** he emphasizes that the main aim of capital punishment is to allow individuals to carry out "catharsis," which Mencken informally defines as "a healthy letting off of steam." **Moreover**, the author believes that everyone feels vengeful at some point. He asserts that "for crimes involving the deliberate and inexcusable taking of human life, to nine men out of ten, capital punishment is a just and proper punishment." This *uncredible* statistic reiterates Mencken's ethos as humorist. Who says nine of ten? It **further** shows that he is not an expert on the judicial system and is just a regular citizen, which brings in more pathos, making him relatable to his audience. **Overall,** the author's satire puts readers at ease with a very serious topic, and that alone may spur Mencken's audience to consider a new perspective.

Choose a prompt and practice GRAB, GAB, GLUE, GOODBYE. Ponder the prompt. Then jot down

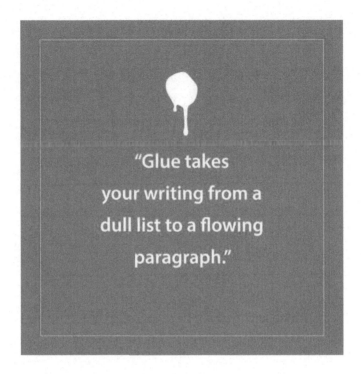

"Glue takes
your writing from a
dull list to a flowing
paragraph."

ideas. Check to see which ones you like most. You
can't have *too many*. While you are writing, avoid
using a word more than once in a paragraph. Look up
a synonym for the second use of the word and plug it
into the sentence instead. *Example:* Too many crooks
do not give their crimes enough thought, or they
would probably change their minds about committing
crimes. (Here, you would find a synonym for the
word "crime" and use it the second time. Some
synonym choices for "crime" are: transgression,

misdeed, felony, offense.) You enhance an essay immediately when you stop repeating words.

Write a Paragraph on Courage

Think of a book you've read that has the theme "courage." What could be better than *Wonder*, by R.J. Palacio? (If you haven't read it, *please do*. You'll love this story.)

Here's the prompt: What can a sport teach a person about courage?

Use this topic sentence:

<u>Basketball can teach people how to work hard when the desire to give up is strong and courage is scarce.</u> Similarly, in the novel *Wonder*, by R.J. Palacio, the hero Auggie Pullman is determined to make friends even though the odds are against him. Referring to people's harsh judgments of his unusual appearance, Auggie wishes that "every day could be Halloween. We could all wear masks all the time. Then we could walk around and get to know each other before we got to see what we looked like under the masks" (Palacio 73). His comment reflects the kind of thinking someone needs when learning to play basketball. It is important for a player not to give up just because he or she feels inferior to other players. A better answer is coming up with clever solutions to troubles.

As you read the student sample, spot the GRAB, GAB, GLUE, and GOODBYE.

Finally, when you have proofread your essay and corrected typos, glance back over it one last time to identify all four Gs. Read it aloud to make sure the GLUE you've selected is enough to add flow to your paragraph(s). Also, check to ensure that you've included sufficient support for the topic sentences with relevant GAB evidence. Another good end step is rereading your teacher's instructions. Have you done everything possible to fulfill essay requirements?

With *Epic Essays* in front of her, author Melissa Mead does final proofreading as she exercises.

Chapter Five:
Steer Skillfully

Tip for the Day: Brainstorm. Ask if your classmates are struggling to find Internet bandwidth or electronic devices at home for academic use. If so, let teachers know about the needs of classmates who are too shy to speak up, especially those suffering from back-in-the-classroom jitters.

Read. To become a good writer, read carefully. Also, study what makes a certain writer's sentences touch you. Is it the rhythm? Do you like that some sentences are super-short, while others are long and winding? Write down some of your favorite sentences as you read. When you come across colorful figurative language (metaphors, similes, personification), underline these in your book—or put them in your Good Writing Journal.

Automatic Steering of your Autopilot Essay is based on who, what, where, when, why, and how. Where is your writing placed? When did the thoughts occur to you? Why are you writing about this topic? How does it affect you? What is the topic? Whom does the topic involve? For an essay to make sense, you must include some of this factual information. Remember that your audience may not have read the text that you reference. Thus, you must clarify how your GAB quote fits in and supports the topic sentence.

When you write an essay, you choose a topic and then argue or advance an idea by analyzing, interpreting facts, or explaining ideas based on research. You use an introduction, body, and conclusion. In particular, most important for high school writers to master are the expository essay, the persuasive (argumentative) essay, and the analytical essay.

Expository: This essay is an informative piece of writing that analyzes a topic by presenting both sides of an issue. You use facts, statistics, and examples. Expository writing encompasses the compare-and-contrast essay, cause-and-effect essay, and the "how to" essay. In these, you do not reveal your personal opinion or write in the first person.

Persuasive: The persuasive (argumentative) essay also presents facts, but the goal is to convince the reader to accept your view or idea. You support your case with examples and evidence, and you also give both sides of the argument. Most important, you seek to persuade the audience that your way is the right way. Again, you cannot use first or second person to make your case. Stick to third person.

Analytical: A perfect example of an analytical essay is the rhetorical essay. Essentially, this is a high-level essay that uses rhetorical appeals (pathos, ethos, logos, kairos) to assess a work of literature.

Narrative essays are entirely different from a formal essay. Narrative writers can use first-person "I" and contractions. Descriptive essays and narrative essays appear commonly in magazines, newspapers, and online (see Part IV of this book for examples).

Certifiably Crazy-about-Writing

One great part about essay writing is that the process helps you finetune skills that you will use throughout your education *and* your profession. You read, write, think, research, and communicate. Essay writing also teaches you to convey information reliably, builds your vocabulary, and strengthens your writing style and voice.

Anyone willing to practice can become a proficient writer. That puts you in a great position for writing research papers, course work, and dissertations. Also, essay writing can help you become a more discerning consumer of information. With "fake news" in the wind and on the Internet, it is important to become a good sorter of information when you're preparing to write and even when you're not. Try to develop critical thinking skills that enable you to ponder an issue, take a side, and argue your point. Naturally, the analytical process gives you another gift, and that's greater respect for other people's perspectives and views.

Believe it or not, someday in corporate America, you'll need to know how to write and spell and communicate. When that day comes, you'll be glad that you know how to write complete sentences and avoid run-ons and fragments. The simple fact that you have writing skills is an advantage in the workplace because you will stand out among job seekers if you're a competent writer. Conversely, if your resume and cover letter are full of typos and grammatical errors, you probably won't be the candidate who wins the position.

What Do You Know about Underdogs?

To practice, write a short paragraph on underdogs. Let's assume this is an unfamiliar topic to you. You think: *I know nothing about this!* That makes it a good idea to start by checking the dictionary definition. Then come up with a topic sentence that explains what you are setting out to show or prove. Your teacher also asks you to include a quote (GAB) from the book your class is reading—*Of Mice and Men*, by John Steinbeck.

Sophomore Josh Martin Hardin writes this topic sentence: <u>An underdog is the team or competitor who is not expected to win, and this is the opposite of being the favorite.</u>

That is your GRAB. Now let your thoughts fly. Write down some good points. What would it feel like to be the underdog in life? In a sports competition? In an academic competition? In ballroom dancing finals?

Next, locate evidence to support your topic sentence. This is GAB.

GAB: (Here's the paragraph that sophomore Josh Martin Hardin writes for this prompt.)

Typically, being named "underdog" has a demoralizing effect. In fact, a person who is not predicted to win a competition may experience low confidence after being called an underdog, or, on the

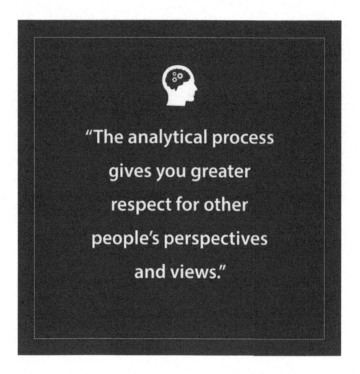

"The analytical process gives you greater respect for other people's perspectives and views."

other hand, it may motivate that individual to overcome the stigma of not being the predicted winner and perform better than expected. In the novel *Of Mice and Men*, written by John Steinbeck, the character Lennie goes through life as an underdog because an intellectual disability limits his social skills. Steinbeck writes that a man "don't need no sense to be a nice fella" (Steinbeck 41). Underdogs like Lennie are basically stuck with their positions in the hierarchy of life, and that means they need friends to watch their backs. In some cases, the underdog designation motivates a person.

You Can Do It!

Test drive your new skills by writing three paragraphs on Britney Spears's lawsuit against her father.

<u>**GRAB:**</u> This is what you claim to be true, and it serves as your topic sentence.

<u>Singer Britney Spears thinks her father meddled in her life when he went to court in 2008 and won the right to manage her money, and her goal is to have a judge lift that order.</u>

The GRAB hooks your reader. With an attention-grabbing topic sentence, you "promise" readers what they are going to get out of reading what you have written.

<u>**GAB for your body paragraph.**</u> Use a GAB quote from a text to support your claim.

In an article from *Page Six* website, Spears complains that it makes her sad to be under restraints "with all the lawyers and doctors and people analyzing me every day." <u>Apparently,</u> the scrutiny of the courts contributes to Spears's unhappiness, and that is unfortunate for a woman who has two children to raise ("Britney Spears Conservatorship")

<u>**GOODBYE:**</u> Wrap up the point you are making.

This is your third paragraph.

<u>Hence,</u> Spears wants her lawyer to get rid of the conservatorship. She argues that she is healthy and financially responsible ("Britney Spears Conservatorship").

GLUE: Check to see that you have "glued" the sentences together so that they flow. Underlined in the above essay are the GLUE words and phrases this student writer used.

A Lion of a Challenge

Now, let's turn to a literature classic. Your class has just finishing reading the novel *Great Expectations*, by Charles Dickens, and the teacher asks everyone to choose a courage quote from that book and use it for the GAB part of an essay.

Here is the prompt: Would having a real lion for a student make Miss Marcy Smith appreciate her human students more?

Check out the paragraph one eighth-grader wrote:

Having a student who is an actual lion makes Miss Marcy Smith more appreciative of her human students for several reasons. To start with, Miss Smith really, truly dislikes seeing students refuse to work hard. However, when a "lion student" bares its teeth right in her face in the classroom, she feels emotions that are far worse than annoyance. Much like the character Pip in *Great Expectations*, facing a real threat puts lesser problems in perspective. Pip actually trembles when he talks with Estella because this haughty older girl enjoys making him feel unimportant. Similarly, Miss Marcy Smith shakes in fear when the "lion" roars, traumatizing her. Finally, she decides that maybe her human students, despite their flaws, deserve appreciation. At least, she does not have to worry that one of them will bite her head off. The moral of the story is that sometimes it takes an ominous threat to humble a person and make that individual recognize blessings.

In the above paragraph, where is GRAB? GAB? GLUE? GOODBYE? Did you find a global statement anywhere?

Chapter Six:
Maximize Your Voice

Tip for the Day: Think of one bad habit you developed during Distance Learning. Did you become a madcap gamer, unable to control your compulsion? If so, this may now be a quasi-addiction, and you should ask a teacher or counselor for help. This is a hard trap to escape, and the yen for frenzied cyber gaming you did during the pandemic won't go away just because you're back in school. How do you plan to handle your super-drive-urge-to-game?

"I like your voice."

You develop your "author's voice" by reading

and writing. This doesn't mean an alto or baritone singing voice. A *writer's* voice refers to how that author comes across on paper: Strong, loud, calm, decisive, or funny, "authorial voice" is how you sound as a writer that celebrates the joy of being you—and yes, you *are* every bit as special as you've been thinking—*secretly, of course.*

"You're really developing a strong voice."

"You need to have your own distinctive voice as a writer…"

The first time you heard these words, you probably Googled "voice." Then you got even more confused. Two kinds of voice exist in writing, and one has nothing to do with the other. Both, though, are important. We'll get to *active and passive voice* later. For now, though, we'll fill you in on the most superb part of essay writing—using your voice. This is the candy store of essay writing, and you can pick up anything you want and snack on it. Enjoy!

You, the Author—Woo-Hoo!

"Authorial voice" springs from your writer persona. You'll love learning this part because it's all about you. You start developing a voice by learning *not* to second-guess every sentence you write, that always ends with the accidental ditching of some of your best ideas.

In teaching writing, an instructor loves reading the original thoughts that spring from every child, and that is why a writer must indulge both the harsh aspects of his psychic recall as well as the lovely-cheery parts. In other words, don't assume that every thought or memory you write has to be "happy" for your teacher to like it. As an example, in my memoir, I tell a story of trips my family took to visit my aunt and uncle in Jennings, Louisiana, where I would gaze in awe at their two daughters' antique dolls cozily housed in a small closet space under the spiral staircase. "You can't touch them," ten-year-old Emily cautioned me one day when she saw the yearning in my eyes. Wait. Was she really saying that a genuine doll lover could only look, not touch? *What kind of torture chamber is this place?* I wondered. Were these really just dolls to admire but not ones to undress, redress, and chop off their hair? Were these beautiful toys designed to torment? These are the kinds of scenes you can revisit when you write—not just the pretty swings under the huge oak trees, where I also played with this cousin, who was actually a great girl. No, the maudlin, miserable bottom feeder in a writer must grovel in some gut-level, heart-wrenching disappointment, or what depths have you probed? It's a scavenger hunt, lifelong, to choose the agonies and ecstasies that will have to come out, revealed in the most sensationally touching prose you've ever written. Especially in writing narrative essays, you can't be afraid to "go there," and you can't sugarcoat every event, trying to convince readers that you really did *have it all*, just like you labor to prove on social media. Unleash the real beast, the real braggart, the real crybaby in you—and then throw off those rusty chains that have kept you bound and worried about what people will think. By the way, for a memoir or personal narrative, you get to abandon the rules of formal essays (see Part IV).

Think of Miguel Cervantes's audacity in his novel *Don Quixote* when he says in the prologue: "I don't have to swear any oaths to persuade you that I should like this book, since it is the son of my brain, to be the most beautiful, elegant and intelligent book imaginable…." (Cervantes 11). If that opener doesn't make a reader want to meet this character, what would? Truly, Cervantes reaches out and captivates so that eons later, his fascinating voice still makes 1000+ pages readable.

Indeed, seeing the world through this author's unique mind keeps the point of view relevant. (Don Quixote gets to use "I" and "you" because this is a narrative tale.) We will never, ever know Cervantes personally, but his famed character Don Quixote, tilting at windmills, makes us wish we could. Writing a book that is notable for experimental form as well as literary playfulness is no small feat, and that in itself makes readers curious about Cervantes.

Then again, what we want to do here is help you, as a writer, maximize *your voice*. Develop your own unique writing style. This is important in nonfiction (essays, articles) and fiction (short stories, novels, poems). After all, the reason we first fall in love with the writing of certain authors is a voice that speaks to us—*touches* us. That is why the process of developing a distinctive style and voice of your own is ultimately very gratifying.

Even one sentence can be provocative. "The highest form of generalship is to balk the enemy's plans" (*The Art of War*, 15 Tzu). In eleven words, the author draws you in and makes you want to know more about the character. *That* is voice. Tzu in 6th century B.C. says emphatically, "He who exercises no forethought but makes light of his opponents is sure to be captured by them" (41 Tzu).

We all know how it feels when a book nudges us to read more of that writer's work—and more—and more. Remember the first time you read a Harry Potter book and that fascinating world pulled you in? *That* is voice. J.K. Rowling's fast-moving storytelling engages, and the strange world she describes so fetchingly and inhabits so reliably with interesting characters keeps you yearning for more.

Sometimes, in fact, a writer's voice is so extraordinary that it is instantly recognizable. Edgar Allan Poe's malevolent voice stands out because he was an expert at keeping readers intrigued. Similarly affecting is Stephen King, author of *Carrie, Christine, The Shining,* and many more novels, who has an authorial voice you can spot by pace, words, and style. Think about it while you're reading a book of his, and you'll notice he casts a spell and narrates in such an enthralling way that readers cannot put the book down even when it's time to stop reading and do something else. He is a master storyteller; his *style* is page-turning, not just the content.

The classics, too, have voices that live forever. When I first read *Jane Eyre,* by Charlotte Bronte, I was fifteen, but the book's inroads on my heart made this novel memorable. Passages such as this arouse curiosity in readers (1874): "While I paced softly on, the last sound I expected to hear in so still a region, a laugh, struck my ear. It was a curious laugh; distinct, formal, mirthless. I stopped: the sound ceased, only for an instant; it began again, louder: for at first, though distinct, it was very low. It passed off in a clamorous peal that seemed to wake an echo in every lonely chamber; though it originated in one, and I could have pointed out the door whence the accent issued" (122).

The haunting tone unnerves the reader. Then, adding richness, the author offers a sneak peek into the era's strict attitude toward children, who were meant to be seen, not heard. Consider this paragraph: "Jane, I don't like...questioners: besides there is something truly forbidding in a child taking up her elders in that manner. Be seated somewhere; and until you can speak pleasantly, remain silent" (13).

Times have changed, and so has child-rearing (thank God).

These teens peer-edit essays.

Unleash Your Voice

To find your voice, check out a piece of writing you've done recently. OR: Write a quick paragraph on a prompt (try this one): *The first day of school in the fall is exciting.* Now, look at what you wrote, and try to be as objective as possible. Pretend you're a young teacher or parent taking a first look at this writing.

Roll your head around on your neck. Throw your arms into the air and wiggle them. Move your shoulders back and forth, as if you're getting ready for a boxing match. Or slap your thighs like an Olympic swimmer. Now examine your writing again. Put on your Critic's Hat (baseball cap or beanie). And, check out these basics of voice:

1) *Speed:* Does your writing move at a fast, explosive pace, or does it build slowly? The sentences you write—are they short, long, or both?

2) *Tone.* Are your words serious, whimsical, modern, old-fashioned, hard-hitting?

3) *Words:* Do you use slang or are you more into old-fashioned, bookish vocabulary? Do you reveal your extensive vocabulary? Do you repeat certain words too often? Circle any that you repeat in this piece of writing you're reviewing. Twice is too much.

4) *Mood*: Study the "feel" or "mood" of your writing. Is your writing so serious it sounds like a passage from a standardized test? Are your sentences too long for a reader to understand? Do lots of short sentences make your writing boring? Do you use formal words or trendy words? For example, in the book *Uglies*, author Scott Westerfeld uses slang, which becomes a key element in building a world that the reader enjoys. Again, ask yourself: *Does my own writing sound like me or someone else?* In creating a voice, you're telling readers, "Welcome to my world!"

Consider these aspects of your personality and demeanor:

Your speed. Are you a ball of energy, rushing around the classroom or your home? If so, you probably favor fast-track writing. Most of your sentences will be short, but you'll link them with the "glue" of transition words. On the other hand, if you're slower and more methodical in movements, you may lean toward longer sentences. If so, throw in some short ones to dilute the heavy syrup on your "essay pancake." Experiment with speed!

Your personality. Are you funny? Outspoken? Quiet and thoughtful? Shy and moody? Loud and outgoing? Quirky and off-the-wall? Your tone-of-spoken-language spills over into your writing and shows your personality. Never fight an inner self that says, "Hey, go ahead and show the world what you're *really, really, really* like." Experimenting with personality writing can be very exciting.

Your clothing: Are you fancy or basic? Do people call you a fashionista or a jock or something else equally descriptive? Take in the comments. Translate that "look" to a writing style. You'll have literally *tons* of choices, and you will have fun sampling what works for you and what doesn't.

Experiment

What will your voice be? Maybe, if you write decoratively, this is a topic sentence you might use: *Author John Steinbeck's writing is uplifting and beguiling, and that keeps the reader engaged.* On the other hand, maybe you favor serious words: *It is clear that readers will find John Steinbeck's writing engaging in regard to simple, heart-stirring emotion.*

Some writers like to mix slang and academic lingo: *At times, the character Scout Finch in* To Kill a Mockingbird, *by Harper Lee, grabs the reader's soul with her youthful observations as well as her serious narration that speaks to the disturbing prejudice in her hometown.*

See? It's all about uncovering you. No more

trying to give the teacher a "regular" person just to play it safe. Believe me, when you deliver the voice inside you, that is the moment you will love writing. After that, you'll welcome the days when your teacher says it's time to write an essay. You'll think: "Here's a chance to have fun, relax, and show my style" instead of what you used to think: "*Oh, man,* I can't write—I hate this!"

When you're writing a first draft, focus on doing two things: (1) write and (2) dream. Have no worries about grammar or anything else that holds you back. Walk it forward. Later is the time to clean up; in second and third drafts, check grammar, contractions, voice, sentence structure, and spelling. Let your voice choose the way the essay goes.

Rock Your Style

Think about the kinds of writing you love when you are reading books. Are you a fan of long descriptions? Does your attention ramp up when the author turns personable, and it feels almost like you're sitting there sharing stories? Ask yourself: How can *I* engage readers? How can I talk about a topic—let's say college-admissions anxiety—in a way that will resonate with teens?

If something resonates, that just means it hits home; you read it and say, "Wow, I've felt that before" or "I get what she's saying…" Try your best to resonate with readers, and you'll soon see an A+ on that essay. More importantly, you'll take pride in having written well.

Example: "Grief comes in waves, paroxysms, sudden apprehensions that weaken the knees and blind the eyes and obliterate the dailiness of life" (Didion, Joan, p. 27, *The Year of Magical Thinking.* Vintage Books, A Division of Penguin Random House LLC: New York. 2005. © Excerpt reproduced with permission of Penguin Random House LLC©*).*

Didion's words resonate with anyone who has experienced bereavement. It is an example of reaching down deep to express the profound sadness that comes with losing a partner-in-life—in Joan Didion's case, her husband.

A Stylish Voice

Most people enjoy writing that has a stylish delivery. After finishing a perfect essay or book, the satisfaction that comes with reading something that touches your heart makes you sigh or smile or both. *Yes,* you think; that's exactly how I feel. On the other hand, you also enjoy writing with some punch and some snap. An easy way to accomplish that effect is varying sentence length. Write long ones, with clauses galore, and then add in some shorter sentences.

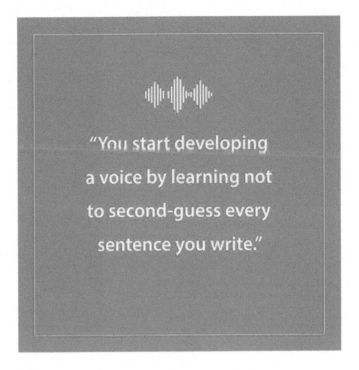

"You start developing a voice by learning not to second-guess every sentence you write."

As a simple rule, *too many* short sentences feel bumpy to readers. Conversely, too many long sentences tire your reader. What works best is using a little of this, a little of that. A little bit country, a little bit rock-and-roll... Just *blend*. No one want to drink a smoothie that has clumps in it, nor is it fun to read an essay that sounds like a clump of unrelated thoughts. Truly, GLUE comes in handy for linking effectively. Memorize a few forms of GLUE, and ever after, you'll have them in your glove compartment anytime you want to pull them out.

Fluff Enough

To color your authorial voice, use adjectives and adverbs, similes and metaphors. Some writing experts argue that too many adverbs and adjectives equal "overwriting," but check out how many authors and columnists use them. No one tells those writers to cut adjectives and adverbs. Do, however, choose active, unusual verbs instead of overusing "is, was, or are." Careful noun and verb choices allow you to discard some adjectives and adverbs, but don't forget—*you* get to choose. Make it reflect *you*. Don't get so minimal that your writing *sounds* the way a bare-of-leaves tree *looks*. Some "decoration" is always good. After all, even the most minimalist room setting in the world has a few color elements that add "pop."

Remember, an essay is nonfiction; *it is real*. A short story is fiction, filled with characters and fantastical "stuff." Parts I and II of *Epic Essays in 30 Minutes* explain how to maximize formal essay writing; Part III adds parents to the mix; Part IV covers personality writing (college entrance essays, narratives, memoirs).

Without emotion, an essay grows chilly. Don't be shy about being an aggressive message-writer. Draw the reader in with the emotional appeal of pathos.

Without your own interpretation of the argument you're making, an essay falls flat. You must persuade readers that your claim stands strong. Use those hard-driving skills that come in handy when you argue with siblings.

By now, you're realizing that formal essay writing is on the serious side, but that doesn't mean it has to be grim. Lilting words, ironic words, and comical images are entertaining. Let ideas spill out onto the paper. Later, scoop up ones you don't like and discard them. Think of your first go-round as pure self-indulgence. Get so loose that you're babbling. Do your wildest yammering ever. Once you feel good about writing essays, you will tend to write and write and write, and it's a spigot that is hard to turn off.

BTW, Toss These

Certain introductions are fine for 6th grade. Just don't use them after that. Examples are the following:

DELETE: I want to tell you.

DELETE: My name is….

"I'm going to write about dogs" is not going to draw in readers. Instead, write "Dogs are man's best friends because they are furry, cuddly, useful, and fun. Take the "I" out of it.

Do not start: "My name is Simon Still, and I want to tell you about peanut farming." That works in elementary school, but now it's important to take your name and "I" out of it.

Your name goes at the top of the page as an identifier. Start your essay by saying:

Peanut farming is harder than most people think it is.

DELETE: I want to tell you.

DELETE: My name is….

Write in 3rd person. *Write in 3rd person.* Oh, did we remember to say *write in 3rd person?* It does not matter that you're actually a gymnast; in a formal essay, you're going to write as if the gymnast were someone else. Get used to third person because this the accepted point of view for formal essays.

Example: Gymnasts understand the importance of hard work.

For your next try, persuade readers that honesty is important. However, keep yourself out of the writing.

Example: Honesty is an important trait. In the long run, most people wind up sorry they took a short cut by cheating.

Obviously, YOU are the one who believes in honesty, but you write so that it sounds like you're talking about "most people" in general. *This means using 3rd person.*

DELETE: I want to tell you.

DELETE: My name is…

DELETE: I think...

NOTE to our readers: For this book, Melissa and I write in first person and second-person conversational style, as if talking with you in your own house. We use "you" and "I" and "we." In essays, though, stick to third person: "he, she, they, it" and "the reader" and "the audience" and "the viewer" (if talking about a video or film). Keep "I" out of essays. Keep "you" out of essays. Or go ahead and write freely—*and then go back and correct these things.*

Super-Swift Takeaways

One of the best ways to develop your writer's voice is reading essays, columns, articles, short stories, novels, and nonfiction books. While reading for content, notice what makes that particular writer "special." Analyze what makes an author's writing compelling. Is it the description? The humor? Does the point of view keep you riveted? Is it so chatty that you feel like the writer is sitting across from you?

Work on your own writing to increase its readability. *Practice.* The more you write and the more you read, the better you will be. Sometimes it takes time to loosen up and believe in yourself, but being young helps because right now you are far more likely to jump off into that mystical writing wonderland than someone older, who has more barriers to being spontaneous.

Keep one happy mantra rolling in your head: **No one on earth has the voice that I have**. A fabulous gift is that one-of-a-kind POV (point of view). When writing paragraphs, remember that *no one* has exactly your perspective on basketball, butternut squash, camping, siblings, greyhounds, or anything else.

Essentially, your individuality makes you the Einstein of your own viewpoint. Hence, erase all negatives running through your brain screaming, "I have nothing to say. I'm just not a writer. It takes me *for-e-ver* to write a paragraph." Those are your worst fears rising up in word form just to be annoying.

Overthinking what you write just superglues *closed* the very mind that you are asking to produce exciting thoughts. Stop putting every sentence under a microscope and wondering if it sounds "silly" or if someone will laugh if your teacher makes you read it. Instead, let it rip; blow minds. Your voice emerges only when you stop binding it in second thoughts.

Great writers do not listen when their minds say, "I wouldn't write that if I were you—it sounds idiotic." If you get too logical and turn your writing into scientific exploration, you will eliminate everything that makes your writing explode off the page and fascinate readers. Just let your thoughts come out, unedited. Be the squeezed orange.

In all likelihood, your final-product essay will surprise even you because it sounds so fresh, so inventive. You'll read it and realize why overediting would have been a mistake. Just like the original maker of Toll House Chocolate-Chip Cookies didn't second-guess perfection, you have to know when to stop tweaking your "product." Put that last period on your essay the second you are able to say, "I think that works—I'm proud of it."

Whatever you did with writing yesterday is history. Start over, and soon you'll be charging through essays like a zippy Indy driver. Then after you've written a rough draft, be sure to let the words "rest" overnight and give the essay a review in the morning. At that time, you may see something that you can't live with and decide to delete it, or you may just smile and praise your effort. (Typically, an item you decide to eliminate on rereading is the very thing you had doubts about as you wrote it; so, your original instinct was right. It's like putting that striped top with plaid pants—somehow, it's not working for you.)

While reading books and articles and short stories and poems, ponder each writer's authorial voice. Is he funny? Is she thought-provoking? Are they sarcastic? Then read something you've written and identify what makes it "you." If it sounds flat and does not reflect your personality, keep writing until something "you-ish" flows from your mind to the paper, with no editing and no *overthinking*. Then you'll see the possibilities within you.

As you write, avoid overdoing interior monologue (those times when you're talking to yourself). "Show, don't tell" means use action-description that explains why giving a dog too many treats can result in pet obesity—or why your older sister's histrionics prove that "first love can make a person insane." Wrap up by saying, "Because of lost love, Jane crumbled." Or: "Rover snacks all day long, and now he is waddling instead of walking."

Every young person has something to say that enchants readers. Remember this. In fact, teachers are quick to say that the most genuine thoughts often come from their "kids" at school. "I've saved all the notes that my students have written me," says Melissa Mead, who teaches English in San Antonio, Texas. "They're priceless."

In developing your writer's voice, keep it as true to you as your brown-gray eyes. Experiment just to see what kind of "voice" sounds best. Ask Mom, Dad, sibling, or friend to give you an opinion. Your question is this: "Which of these paragraphs sounds most like it came from me?"

Don't try to be Pharrell Williams or John Green or Steven Spielberg. The goal is to be *you* because that's your source of original thoughts. Most important, don't worry about getting your writing perfect. That isn't necessary. Besides, trying to be perfect hurts you.

Xanthe Shirley, a young entomologist in College Station, Texas, recalls that seeking perfection cramped her writing for years. "It was like a huge anchor weighing down my creativity and making my writing sound robotic. Then I took a writing workshop at A&M University and learned to unload thoughts and then go back later for a second and third look. I was no longer held hostage by 'the thought police,' who were telling me I had to write perfectly. Now I write with ease."

Be bold, Xanthe Shirley recommends. "If you like ironic words or clever images, use them. Let ideas spill onto paper. Later, go back and cut ones you don't like." On the first go-around, though, be a free spirit of self-indulgence. If you are witty, show off your sense of humor in your writing. If you write in a sophisticated, highbrow way, go in that direction. Let your language reflect you and your awesome mind.

And, to reiterate, never skip the cold-storage test. Glance at an essay you wrote the day before and let chill overnight, and you'll see that the best parts were those you let flow freely. If the roar of the crowd in your head limits you, wear earmuffs (figurative ones or even literal ones). Allow yourself to write without inhibitions, and your second review of your own work will have you saying, "Wow, did I write that? It's really good!"

What Is Your Brand?

How do you broadcast yourself? What is your "why"? Really, in order to create a good brand online, you can't blather on and on. Think of the many times you've been on social media and a friend just won't shut up, and you want to yell "enough!" Always leave your readers wanting more. Usually, the yada-yada-yada parts should stay in the *yada pile*—unsaid but just inferred.

Is your social media or Internet voice the one you want to use in school essays? Does it move your message? Or is it too casual to fit in an academic framework?

Here's the kicker: you *can* have different authorial voices for different platforms. In addition, keep in mind that borrowing some of your ruthless wit from social media posts when crafting a savvy essay will bring life and personality to your argument, and it will show more of *you, the writer.*

Now, as you read the following examples, pinpoint what makes these voices special:

"The boys had a long talk, but it brought them

little comfort. As the twilight drew on, they found themselves hanging about the neighborhood of the isolated jail, perhaps with an undefined hope that something would happen that might clear away their difficulties. But nothing happened; there seemed to be no angels or fairies interested in this luckless captive" (Twain, *Huckleberry Finn* 152). *The reference to "no angels or fairies interested" is spot-on in helping readers vicariously experience the inevitable doom.*

"When I tell you that a tiny vitamin supplement, a little sun, and some dietary fixes can alter your health dramatically, I bet you'll shake your head with skepticism" (Dowd, Stafford 2). *Alluding to readers shaking their heads is a good visual that livens up this self-help book.*

"Yet, despite his appearance, he was really a very complicated young man with a whole set of personalities, one inside the other like a nest of Chinese boxes" (West). *Here, Nathaneal West, author of* The Day of the Locust, *creates a fascinating metaphorical picture that readers identify as being like someone they know who has so many facets that it is impossible to know the man well; he is a total enigma.*

"The man had to touch him twice on the shoulder before he woke, and as he opened his eyes a faint smile passed across his lips, as though he had been lost in some delightful dream. Yet he had not dreamed at all. His night had been untroubled by any images of pleasure or of pain. But youth smiles without any reason. It is one of its chiefest charms" (Wilde 143).

In the excerpt above, consider the effectiveness of the last two sentences—the provocative observation that one of youth's best charms is smiling "without any reason."

"The brightly colored <u>parasols danced and dipped like monstrous butterflies</u>" (Wilde 61). *Notice the underlined simile and the excellent picture it creates instantly.*

"'If everybody married the person they love...parents would lose their power to marry their children when and to whom they should; and if it were left to daughters to choose their husbands as they pleased, one would pick her father's servant, and another a man she has seen walking down the street and who she thinks looks jaunty and dashing, even though he is in reality some wild swashbuckler; because love and fancy easily blind the eyes of understanding, which are so necessary when making decisions about settling down in life, and with marriage there is such a danger of making mistakes... when a prudent man sets out on a long journey, he first looks for someone trustworthy and agreeable to keep him company. Well, should not someone setting out on the journey of life, with death as his destination, do the same, particularly since the person he chooses will keep him company in bed, at the table and everywhere else, as a wife does her husband?' said Don Quixote" (611).

Notice Cervantes's style of winding, meandering sentences that somehow keep the reader's interest. This is fascinating when you consider the publication dates of Don Quixote, *in two parts in 1605 and 1615.*

"He had passed visibly through two states and was entering upon a third. After his embarrassment and his unreasoning joy, he was consumed with wonder at her presence. He had been full of the idea so long, dreamed it right through to the end, waiting with his teeth set, so to speak, at an inconceivable pitch of intensity. Now, in the reaction, he was running down like an overwound clock (Fitzgerald 91-92, excerpt from *The Great Gatsby*©, by F. Scott Fitzgerald, reproduced with permission of The Licensor through PLSclear©).

In the above excerpt from The Great Gatsby, *note the simile (underlined) and the long sentences that come to an abrupt halt.*

See how easy it is to study an author's style while you are reading for content? Make a habit of this, and you'll improve your writing as you soak up the sensory impact and emotional aspects of texts.

Chapter Seven:
Accelerate Automatically

Tip for the Day: Repair the "social backsliding" that happened during COVID days. Sure, it wasn't your fault that kids were held in solitary confinement for a year and a half, but now it is up to you, as a young adult, to find ways to gravitate away from the social straitjacket that became your everyday fate. Get in the driver's seat. You are no longer isolated. View social opportunities as chances to upgrade and take advantage.

    Shift into "drive." Now that you know the basics, pick up speed. Expand your vocabulary and develop your writing style. Relax and take a few deep breaths.

Being too rigid in writing equates to driving while pumping the brake. So, cruise and smile. Think of the world of possibilities in front of you. Words and thoughts flow more easily when you stop worrying about formatting, outside opinions, dinner options, printer cartridges, and other things that can slow you down.

Today is your writing do-over. You're no longer going to scratch your head and complain that you don't know what to write. Your mind is full of ideas and thoughts, and you're ready to write them down. In fact, you probably have too many to include in one essay.

Imagine, for example, that your teacher asks you to write about what makes mariachi bands popular. Maybe your first thought is: "How am I supposed to know anything about that?" Fine. Your second thought will be: "I'll research this, and then write a sentence that says what I want to prove or argue." If you've never heard a mariachi band, find a YouTube video, and listen and watch; absorb the feel and flavor of mariachi music.

Write a topic sentence that goes something like this: <u>Mariachi bands are popular because their cheerful, bouncy music makes people happy.</u> Follow up with more explanation: <u>Event planners often choose these bands for celebrations because festive</u>

music puts audiences in the mood for having fun. In your topic sentence, or GRAB, you tell readers what you hope to prove or explain or persuade. Then follow up with examples.

After doing a few minutes of online research on mariachi bands, list items you want to include in your paragraph. Consider these:

- Historically, mariachis provide music for traditional Latino celebrations.

- At the party that Latino families host for a teen girl's celebration of maturity, a band plays, and typically, the music-makers are mariachis. The *quinceañera* marks a girl's 15th birthday, and it is common for people in Mexico, Latin America, the Caribbean, and Latino communities in the U.S. to celebrate this religious and social event ("*Quinceañera*," Britannica).

- People expect to hear mariachi bands at Mexican weddings, *quinceañera*s, birthday parties, civic celebrations, baptisms, funerals, and serenades, and for that reason, hiring a band is usually part of the event budget.

- Many Mexican-Americans grow up loving the prospect of enjoying mariachis at cultural functions.

- These bands wear traditional costumes:

"elegant snugly tailored black suit and vest brightly trimmed in silver buttons and embroidery and worn with a soft tie, and wide-brimmed sombrero" (Mariachi Plaza Directory and Service Center).

- Instruments include: guitar, *vihuela* (a fretted, plucked Spanish string instrument, shaped like a guitar but tuned like a lute), *guitarron* (large bass guitar), violins, trumpets, and the groups play rancheras, corridos, cumbias, boleros, ballads, *sones, huapangos, jarabes, chotis, joropos, pasodobles*, marches, polkas, and waltzes ("*Quinceañera*," Wikipedia).

- Many Mexican restaurants have strolling mariachis who entertain diners.

- Though male mariachis dominate the field, female mariachi bands are also extremely popular.

From researching this topic, you learn that this traditional type of band has roots that go back to Jalisco, Mexico, with the richness of Spanish culture evident in the music, costumes, and instrumentation. *Mariachi* refers to "musicians who dress and play in a style typical of the Mexican state of Jalisco, although the style and music played have spread far beyond the limits of Jalisco and *jalisciense* music itself" (Mariachi Plaza Directory and Service Center).

Now you have *too much* material for a short essay. Sort and choose. Glance over facts and decide which ones you want to include. Then tweak your topic sentence into a GRAB that promises readers "here's what I'm going to tell you." And be sure you fulfill that promise.

A high school sophomore wrote the following paragraph. He underlines the topic sentence.

Mariachi bands are popular because their cheerful, bouncy music makes people happy, but what makes them actual institutions of the Mexican culture are the instruments, costumes, music, and history. Still, the main reason event planners choose mariachis to play at events is that these bands' festive music puts audiences in the mood for having fun. As Californian Renzo Gregorio Sanchez says, "I grew up enjoying mariachis at weddings and parties, and as a boy, I always wished I could have a complete costume, from sombrero to embroidered vest. My whole family associated the happy music with good times." For band members to produce their infectious music, it takes a number of instruments, including a guitar, *vihuela* (a fretted, plucked Spanish string instrument shaped like a guitar), *guitarron* (large bass guitar), violins, and trumpets. Furthermore, the kinds of music that the mariachis play with such gusto are: *rancheras, corridos, cumbias, boleros,* ballads, *sones, huapangos, jarabes, danzones, joropos, pasodobles,* marches, polkas, waltzes, and *chotís* ("*Quinceañera,*" Wikipedia). Today, many Mexican-Americans would be disappointed to attend an event without a mariachi band because these are such special elements in celebrations, from baptisms to funerals, birthday parties to *quinceañeras.* For example, most Latinos expect to hear heart-pounding mariachi serenades at a *quinceañera,* which is a religious and a social event toasting the life of a fifteen-year-old girl as she goes from childhood to adulthood ("*Quinceañera,*" *Britannica*). In the end, though, the most memorable part of mariachi entertainment is the delightful enthusiasm of the performers, who capture the essence of Mexican celebration in costumes and music. Thus, mariachi audiences always cherish these musicians, and non-Latinos end up wishing their own cultures had similarly joyful bands.

Styling Your Essay

How do you give an essay "style"? This an area that Gwen Gaylord, AP/IB English teacher in Newport Beach, California, considers "the most difficult element to 'teach,'" she says. "It's ineffable but so important and can really only be learned through reading, reading, reading!"

Style also goes hand in hand with authorial voice.

When Gwen Gaylord comes across a student who shows a developing voice, she nurtures that ability. Furthermore, she helps her students tighten up their essays and eliminate material that does not support the topic sentence. "Sometimes it's challenging for young writers to see the parts that are off track versus the ones that should be included," she says

A good teacher also knows how critical praise is to each student's growth. Otherwise, she or he will have a hard time getting that teen to focus and learn simply because hopelessness prevails when the child enters that class. In a peer edit or a parent review, try to find something noteworthy. No student wants to think there was nothing of merit in an entire essay.

Reading for Style

As you read, assess what makes a certain piece of writing noteworthy. *Example:* "She generally gave herself very good advice (though she very seldom followed it)." This memorable sentence comes from author Lewis Carroll's novel *Alice's Adventures in Wonderland / Through the Looking-Glass.*

Yes, you *have* to smile at this relatable thought. Who hasn't ignored that little voice within? You like what Lewis Carroll says about human nature. Similarly, you have thought of something clever like that but kept it to yourself. Now, though, you see clearly that an essay can showcase some of your richest thoughts. That's how those writers whose books you read in English class *became* writers. One day they sensed that their one-of-a-kind observations were extraordinary and decided to share them.

Going Down Style Lane

Read the paragraph below and enjoy the similes (underlined).

"One way that propaganda campaigns in Europe and the United States activated public sentiment was by using animals. <u>Depicting the nations at war as animals</u>, propaganda artists bred sympathy for allies and fear of foes. A series of French postcards, for example, show the <u>Allied Powers as elegant butterflies with the faces of beautiful young women</u>. Dressed in national costume and sporting wings tinted in the colors of their national flags, the graceful creatures are gentle and fragile. <u>The Central Powers, on the other hand, were depicted as stinging wasps and scaly beetles,</u> with the faces of stern-faced old men, each symbolically slain with a sword and pinned to paper <u>as if it were a dead specimen in an entomology collection</u>" (Waycott).

In the excerpt below, notice the interesting comparison of Kim Kardashian to Marie Bashkirtseff:

"In May 1884, long before the likes of Kim Kardashian achieved celebrity through the careful curation and promotion of self, a young unknown named Marie Bashkirtseff staked her desire for fame on the publication of her personal diary. She knew she was consumptive and that she had little time left. Her right lung was irrevocably damaged. The left had steadily deteriorated. Bones were now visible where they had not been before. Taking up her pen and a fresh notebook, she composed what would become the definitive version of the preface to her diary" (Wilson).

In the following, note how the writer effectively compares then and now:

"In an era of almost instantaneous communication via email, phone, and social media, it is easy to forget how important correspondence was as a technology to bridge social distance. Letters, as Petrarch's ancient Roman hero Cicero famously declared, made the absent present. The act of correspondence could also, of course, bring anguish. Petrarch worried about whether friends were still alive if they did not respond quickly. 'Free me from these fears as soon as possible by a letter from you,' Petrarch encouraged one of his closest friends...in September 1348. Communication may not have been swift, but it was nonetheless effective and, ultimately, reassuring" (Findlen).

Find the metaphors in the following paragraph.

"It is not a stretch to say that he is among the best writers on democratic freedom. More than anyone, {Sinclair} Lewis understands its aims and its limitations for both individuals and the country. For him, freedom is playful but serious, directionless but purposeful, and essential to knowing true happiness. Lewis sees that kind of freedom as America's greatest virtue and best export. It would be tragic if we were to somehow lose it" (Michaels).

Assessing Style, Tone, Point of View

For essay writing, develop a thorough understanding of style, tone, and point of view. Furthermore, for taking AP exams, SATs, and ACTs, you'll want a good grasp of these terms for multiple-choice, short-answer, and essay questions.

- **Style** refers to a particular author's way of expression; in other words, is he "preachy" or straightforward or emotional?
- **Tone** is the attitude or mood the author's style reveals. One author may be fanciful. Another is ironic. and yet another is pessimistic.
- **Point of view** emerges when style and tone intersect and offer the author's outlook.

Writers use three main perspectives:
- First-person, using "I" and "we"
- Second-person, using "you" and "your"
- Third-person, using "he," "she," or "it," which can be limited—single-character knowledge—or omniscient, which means "all-knowing."

Spot the Signposts

In the following writing, analyze style, tone, and point of view.

The pandemic caused an unbelievably chaotic year in the U.S. People began getting sick with COVID-19 in January 2020, and by March, a nationwide shut-down affected businesses, schools, and most of America for about eighteen months. Peace of mind flew out the window. Many students experienced a sense of gloom and doom that was unprecedented in their lives. Road rage incidents and crimes escalated.

Often it seemed that the entire globe was coming apart at the seams. Family disputes, health meltdowns, and workplace dysfunction exploded until the numbers were so off the charts that healthcare facilities were unable to handle requests for help. People wondered why their leaders could not find answers. *What is wrong with people today? How can one little virus leave so many people unhinged?*

In the end, the freefall of emotions that Americans experienced caused an uptick in mental health issues that lingered even after people were vaccinated and the situation calmed somewhat. It has been a mess. How awful that problems still haunt the U.S. almost two years since the beginning of the pandemic outbreak!

Now, you will try to define the writer's style. Would you call it hard-hitting? Aggressive? Nasty? Define the tone. Brash? Angry? Depressing? Define the point of view. Is the author lashing out? Disgruntled? Cynical? Spiteful?

Choose from these multiple-choice options to characterize the tone of the writer:

a. Accusatory

b. Hateful

c. Backbiting

d. Nihilistic

e. Ironic

There are two you can eliminate quickly. The tone does not seem ironic, and hateful doesn't fit, either. Nihilism means a belief that life is meaningless, which isn't the correct choice because this writer is describing one year only. That leaves backbiting and accusatory, and now you have a hard choice. It does appear that the author is looking for a scapegoat, trying to accuse someone of wrongdoing, but the tone is also backbiting in that it sounds malicious, like the writer is gossiping about people behind their backs. However, since no one person is singled out, the best answer would be "accusatory."

This illustrates how an extensive vocabulary can help you when writing essays and taking exams. On the SAT, for example, you may encounter words that you do not understand, and that prevents you from sorting exam answers well and choosing the right one. In addition, a wide vocabulary is a gigantic asset for writing essays. You simply have more tools, and that leads to a stronger essay, with more swagger and attitude.

Old-Style Voices

In doing online volunteer transcription of old documents for The Smithsonian, Newport Harbor High School senior Adam-Neal Smith was surprised to discover how ornate the English language was in 1800s America. Two interesting facts stood out to him: people were excellent spellers, and they had elegant penmanship (cursive).

"Sometimes it's challenging for young writers to see the parts that are off track versus the ones that should be included."

One example was a letter in which a school superintendent offers a job to a woman who wants to be a teacher, and he writes that her application has been "favorably approved and appreciated," and the district will "look forward to having her joyful countenance and dainty personage in a classroom that fall, when she will partake of the opportunity to instruct children who must be ruled with an iron hand and taught with a cordial voice. Because I know that you have three small children at home, I assume that you have made proper accommodations so that taking care of them in addition to your school position will not be a burden beyond your ability to handle" (The Smithsonian). The principal adds that he has received "extremely glowing accounts of her professionalism and skills, and people proudly attest to her extreme devotion to her students and to teaching."

Obviously, over the decades, starchiness has gone out of writing styles, which makes it incumbent on today's writers to take stock of the precedents they are setting. Staying true to oneself is important, and at no time in history has that been more apparent than today. The Internet welcomes endless opinions, including some that are not worth hearing. The phrase "everybody's a writer" has never had a truer ring, but with that newfound freedom comes responsibility. Thus, strive for moral decency. Write to do good rather than harm.

Can You Evaluate Syntax?

Sentence structure and grammar make up the language term "syntax." What is important is grasping how the manipulation of syntax can make writing more provocative in viewpoint, tone, and meaning. Look at this example from *Don Quixote*, by Cervantes.

"Many weighty histories of knights errant have I read, but never I have read, or seen, or heard of enchanted knights being carried off in this way or as slowly as these heavy, slothful beasts promise; for knights are always borne through the air, at extraordinary speed, wrapped in some dark, grey cloud, or on some chariot of fire, or on some hippogryph[1] or similar beast; but for me to be carried off now on an ox-cart does, as God is good, throw me into the greatest confusion! Yet maybe the chivalry and the enchanting of these times of ours follow different paths from those of earlier days. And it could also be that, since I am a new knight in the world, and the first to resuscitate the forgotten exercise of knight-errantry, new forms of enchantment and other ways of carrying off the enchanted have been invented. What do you think, Santo my son?" (433 Cervantes).

In one of the most-read novels of all times, Cervantes constructs a political allegory that is alternately comical and esoteric. This trailblazing book depicts exploits of a buffoon who goes on a mission to square up reality with fantasies that are

---

[1] The hippogriff, or hippogryph, is a creature whose front half is an eagle and hind half, a horse (Wikipedia).

more appealing. The oxcart anecdote he describes here is just one of many delusions-of-grandeur-gone-awry in Don Quixote's adventures. However organically it emerges from the writer, the syntax of this excerpt is structured to let readers feel the absurdity of his rambling thoughts as he recounts the modest errand of being a "new knight" and "the first to resuscitate knight-errantry" (433). The syntax works with style, tone, and point of view to resurrect for posterity a fanciful-yet-lovably-wacky narrator who tilts at windmills that Quixote mistakes for monsters. The novel's circa-1605 experimental form and literary playfulness take this powerful book from a haphazard allegory to a classic that still straddles the literary world eons later.

Chapter Eight:
Use Gab Quotes

Tip for the Day: Still feeling anxious even though you've been back in the classroom for months? Anxiety disorder is a real thing, and if you are experiencing a deep degree of separation from your classmates and educators, ask your counselor for resources that can help you resolve this problem. You don't have to be upset every day, and there are perfectly good solutions. Asking for help is a great idea, always. Advocate for you! You deserve to find a way to feel happier.

GAB about a book. Choose a text you have read that has a relatable thread, or, in other words, an experience common to many people. Find three books from which you can pull handy allusions for all-purpose essays. Create a "stable" of standbys you can use anytime that they fit.

On the other hand, if your teacher asks you to write about a certain text, that means you must pull quotes from THAT BOOK or poem or short story or play. Only the times that your choice is wide open will you turn to one of your trusty three books.

Understand this: Teachers *love-love-love* allusions (GAB). Allusions make your essay stand out because few students know how to use these. Many high school writers are unaware that allusions make essays stronger. The bottom line is that including allusions is a surefire way to stand out in a traffic snarl of students vying for prominence.

Your Gs for Essay Writing

To cruise down the road, use GRAB, GAB, GLUE, GOODBYE. Four steps:

GRAB: Start with a GRAB sentence that gets the attention of your reading audience.

GAB: For the GAB part, include a RELEVANT quote or two from the book you read (or the reference text you found online). Then tell why the quote matters.

GLUE: Super-stick sentences together with

connecting "glue" words: also, in addition, etc. By studying the options, you will learn where to use each.

GOODBYE: Conclude by mentioning *one more time* what you set out to say and how you proved your point. Think of this part as your wrap-up. When you are finished, check for complete sentences, no run-on sentences, and sentences of different lengths. Shoot for including about seven sentences in your final paragraph.

GRAB-GAB-GLUE-GOODBYE is a snap. Practice till it's second nature. Then you know exactly how to write a basic paragraph or essay.

Write Like No One Is Watching

"Shakespeare, Leonardo da Vinci, Benjamin Franklin and Abraham Lincoln never saw a movie, heard a radio, or looked at television," said poet Carl Sandburg. "They had 'loneliness' and knew what to do with it. They were not afraid of being lonely because they knew that was when the creative mood in them would work" ("Carl Sandburg Quotes").

Look at this quote carefully. What does Sandburg mean by saying these famous people *knew what to do with loneliness*?

For writing your own essay on loneliness, use this topic sentence:

GRAB: It is a sunny summer, and while some

teens are working or beachcombing, others are complaining "I have nothing to do."

GAB: Hit by the reality of being home alone, they do not know what to do with long stretches of time that are not filled with homework or chores. However, they can take a hint from poet Carl Sandburg, who once marveled that even though Shakespeare, Leonardo da Vinci, Ben Franklin, and Abe Lincoln never saw a movie, heard a radio, or watched television, "they were not afraid of being lonely because they knew that was when the creative mood in them would work."

(Note how we *weave* the quote into the sentence, not just plunk it down by itself.)

All right, so you have a GAB quote. Now back it up with some GAB evidence, such as this:

Truly, super-connected Gen Z[2] kids have a hard time settling down alone and often have no idea what to do when a wave of creativity washes over them during solitude. Perhaps that is a great time for them to pull out a writing pad and try peering up at an endless blue sky to see if they can come up with interesting thoughts to write down. If necessary, teens can wrestle with ideas that come to mind until they manage to tie down the best one. Imagine thoughts

---

[2] Gen Z is the generation born 1997-2015. Age range: six to 24, with about 68 million in the U.S. (Wikipedia).

scrambling around, unmanageable as greased pigs in a rodeo, while the teen contestant, determined to rope one, singles out the ideal catch, tosses a rope around it, pulls it to the ground, and wins a scholarship for her efforts. (And the pig goes free!)

Your thoughts are *yours for the taking*. Sample the following prompts and see what ideas they evoke. Enjoy the flashing-in-your-mind thoughts that are funny, serious, outrageous, and spot-on:

- What would Shakespeare say about online dating websites?
- How would Abraham Lincoln perform as a Senator in the U.S. today?
- What would Leonardo da Vinci find fascinating to paint in this era?
- What would Ben Franklin think of cell phones, and what would he invent?

The example below is a freshman's paragraph.

Leonardo da Vinci gets off the plane from time travel and looks around. This is an airport, but all he sees are people looking at small metal items in their hands. *Interesting*, he thinks. Everyone is distracted, studying tiny handheld screens. No one looks at the two people walking right next to them, ignoring those who are closest, probably the very ones who really matter. This reminds Leonardo da Vinci that "sometimes men fail to see what is right in front of them." This means he observes that the blind people walking around him prove that it is true. Perhaps, the objects they love fool them into thinking they have everything they need as long as their battery stays charged, and they fail to understand that the people in close proximity are the most important "items."

Use GAB Effectively

Write an essay on the theme of empathy, acceptance, prejudice, or friendship. For a source of evidence quotes, choose one of the books listed below or another text that deals with one of these topics.

- *The Call of the Wild*, written by Jack London
- *Wonder*, written by R. J. Palacio
- *To Kill a Mockingbird*, written by Harper Lee
- *The Outsiders*, written by S. E. Hinton

When you are writing, REMEMBER:

- Use no contractions (change "can't" to cannot, etc.).
- Use present tense: (Sam moves and yells, not moved and yelled.)
- INCLUDE TAG—title, author, genre.
- Use third person (he, she, they, the reader, the readers, one), and DO NOT use first person (I, we) or second person (you). The

exception? When you use a quote from the text you're studying, "you" or "I" may be part of the quote, and that means you have to leave those words in place.

Note: When you pull a quote from a source to use in your essay, tell the reader the *page number* where it appeared in the original book, play, article, or short story. This is called a citation, which goes *outside* the quotation marks. Example: "It was kind of lazy and jolly, laying off comfortable all day, smoking and fishing, and no books nor study" (Twain 25). In the Works Cited (bibliography) section, you list the full attribution for Mark Twain's novel *Adventures of Huckleberry Finn.*

"In your conclusion, paraphrase the original claim, and mention the evidence you gave to support it."

To show how quickly students can write an Autopilot Essay, sophomore Patrick Graber finishes his in 25 minutes. To test the Autopilot Essay, coauthors Mead and Stafford sampled 62 students in grades 7-12. Of those, 95% finished within the 30-minute time frame. (Three-paragraph Autopilot Essays can serve as first drafts for more in-depth essays.)

As a step up, the Cruise-Control Essay has five paragraphs and takes about 60 minutes to complete. "I liked following the plan," said freshman Joaquin Rigdon. "It's straightforward and fun." His only challenge was reminding himself not to use "you." Patrick Graber said his only difficulty was "keeping it {the essay} in present tense because I'm not used to

that."

Sample Hooks

Practice different kinds of GRAB hooks. Try one that has descriptive words, like this: *Southern California has only one season although some summer days are a little bit cold and some winter days a little bit warm.*

OR: Make readers curious. Example: *Trent Mason zips down Irvine Boulevard away from Seaside High School. Looking back, he sees what he is trying to escape, and that makes him run even faster.*

GAB

Use the VERY IMPORTANT TRICK of tucking the GAB (allusion) into every essay you write. Show that you remember what you have read. When you "allude" with an "allusion," you refer to something. *Example:* Ethan Melton alludes to lessons he learned from the "Wimpy Kid" books.

FACT: You will love-crave allusions when you get used to including them in essays.

GAB possibilities:

- Use Shakespeare's words, such as the old favorite "All's well that ends well."
- Use 19th-century German philosopher Friedrich Nietzsche's aphorism: "What doesn't kill you makes you stronger" (also one of Kelly Clarkson's great songs).

- Use the words of a famous person. Showing his belief in fairness, President Abraham Lincoln once said, "I don't like that man. I must get to know him better" ("Abraham Lincoln Quotes").

Welcoming the GAB

Allusions SUPPORT what you're writing. As a side benefit, they make you sound like a really bright kid, and you *are*, so why not share that with readers? Teachers expect allusions; that's why they ask you to include evidence quotes that support the claim you are making in your essay. We call it GAB!

BEST-KEPT SECRET: If you allude to something (other than the story you are reading for your class), a teacher thinks: "Here's a student who knows how to write." For example, consider a story problem with seemingly no solution. Example: In the short story "The Gift of the Magi," by O. Henry, the reader sees the irony of receiving a gift that cannot be used and giving a gift that requires sacrifice. In this story, there is no satisfying solution. It is fascinating to see the situation go so far off the rails from the original intentions of the givers. In "Magi," the story brings temporary sadness to a husband and wife whose gifts validate their great love. This reminds "Magi" readers of the fairy tale "The Lady, or the

Tiger," by Frank Stockton, which is another story problem with no solution. If you're writing about "Magi" and you refer to "The Lady, or the Tiger," you're using an allusion. For your writing purposes, it is your GAB. Or you can pull a quote from "Magi." An allusion refers to a person, place, thing, or idea, and you, the writer, want readers to spot the allusion and say, "A-hah! I get it!"

Example: "The character Smithy acted like a Romeo when he was around class president Julie Shin." Here, "Romeo" is a reference to Shakespeare's Romeo, lover of Juliet, in the play *Romeo and Juliet.* This GAB allusion communicates by saying that Smithy flirted with Julie.

Write One, Two, or Three Paragraphs

Choose one of these four prompts, and write one, two, or three paragraphs: intro, body, and conclusion.

To gain acceptance from peers, a teen should not have to surrender his or her values.

OR

A quest for friendship is often a part of growing up.

OR

Once teens see how prejudice changes people, it alters their worldview.

OR

Developing empathy requires getting outside of oneself by stretching the muscles of unselfishness and kindness.

Essay Road

Choose a prompt from those listed for your topic sentence. Everything in your essay will support prejudice OR acceptance OR empathy OR friendship. The topic sentence sets out exactly what you intend to argue for the ears of your audience.

Within the topic sentence, include TAG— title, author, and genre. *Example:* In the novel *To Kill a Mockingbird*, by Harper Lee, the character Scout Finch learns that prejudice makes people act in strange ways.

For your second paragraph, write a sentence explaining how the GAB quote illustrates the theme. Example. This might start a second paragraph drawing an evidence quote from a hypothetical (fake) book: *Through his own experiences, camp leader Marshall Lane learns that "too many people judge on appearances even though looks do not begin to reveal the true person" (Lane 3).* Notice how the quote is tucked inside the sentence. By the way, make sure you always use a relevant quote from the book you are reading or another book; the GAB has to *illustrate your claim.* The material you include at the end within parentheses, such as (Lane 3), is called a "citation." You're giving credit for the quote to the author who wrote it and the page number on which the quote was found. For detailed information on citations, go to Purdue Online Writing Lab.

After your GAB quote, write two to three sentences that explain why the GAB quote is important and link it back to supporting the topic sentence (and the theme).

Third paragraph/conclusion: Use the word "Finally," at the start of this concluding sentence or another concluding transition. "Finally, the author conveys his theme of acceptance (or prejudice or friendship or empathy) with examples that show why belonging is important to most people." Again, this sentence must refer back to what the topic sentence discusses.

In your conclusion, paraphrase the original claim and mention the evidence that you gave to support it. Go back and read what you've written. Underline the title of the book or put it in italics. Also, make sure that your entire essay sticks to the one topic you chose, whether it's prejudice, acceptance, empathy, or friendship.

One easy trick that will help you make sure you reiterate the gist of the original topic

sentence or thesis sentence is this: Copy/paste it word for word into your conclusion spot and then paraphrase it. You'll end up with a totally different sentence that still retains the essence of what you planned to prove at the outset.

For essay assignments, you usually will choose quotes from the novel or short story or poem that your class is studying at the time. Just make sure you select ones that support the claim that you are making—not just random quotes. Occasionally, students think their work is done when they just pull out a quote and slip it into their essay. Not so fast there! Remember, the whole purpose of the GAB is to include evidence that basically says to the reader, "See, this shows that what I'm arguing in my topic sentence is correct."

Going on Autopilot

Below is an example of an essay a 7th-grade student wrote, using the Autopilot Essay.

In the novel *The Outsiders*, written by S. E. Hinton, the theme centers around a teen seeking acceptance and coping with difficulties involved. When a person feels like an outsider, the tendency is to look for a welcoming group, and this quest often occurs in adolescence.

Groups are complicated. For example, Ponyboy,

the protagonist in *The Outsiders*, thinks a gang is tough to understand. However, he believes that his friends should let others tell their sides of a story, and then "maybe people would understand and wouldn't be so quick to judge a boy by the amount of hair oil he wore" (Hinton 179). The protagonist wishes people understood that it is wrong to judge people by their appearance, and even though groups do make this mistake, it is wrong. The author conveys the theme of acceptance, and Ponyboy learns the importance of belonging. In the end, though, he sees that true acceptance occurs only when fitting in comes naturally and the person is being genuine.

For Word Warriors

Grab readers. Hook readers. Hold 'em. Your essay starts out by snagging the attention of a teacher, a classmate, a friend, or a parent. Try explaining why people love J. K. Rowling's Harry Potter books, for example. Make your opening a warm "come on in" intro that makes readers smile, as in "yes, I want to read more of this…"

Write a topic sentence for a paragraph. A few ideas that some middle school English students offered as Harry Potter essay GRABs are:

- Fanciful. Fun. Intriguing.
- Harry Potter never meets a puzzle he does not

like.

- Glasses. Robe. Tie. Buttoned-up boy.
- To say Harry Potter is relatable is a huge understatement.
- A good mystery makes the mind itch.

These are GRABS. Note that when the goal is to grab attention at the start of an essay, a complete sentence isn't needed every single time. See numbers 1 and 3. In those cases, the second sentence in the paragraph will be the one with TAG information on the book.

Keep in mind that your paragraph or multi-paragraph essay uses these:

GRAB: Grab your reader's attention with a startling statement. Then, use sentence two to give a promise of what's to come. Tell your readers what the essay will prove or persuade or explain and include the TAG info (title, author, genre).

GAB. Your "gab" supports your promise. Find a quote from the text you are reading and weave it into the essay. Make sure the quote is relevant to your topic; for example, if you are writing about the need for connection with other human beings, pull a quote from John Steinbeck's novel *Of Mice and Men*, and make sure it's one that says something about people connecting. *Example:* The intellectually disabled protagonist is Lennie Small, whose friend George

Milton keeps him out of trouble. One day when they are talking, George refers to the loneliness of life on a ranch, but Lennie thinks he and George are okay "because I got you to look after me, and you got me to look after you, and that's why" (Steinbeck 14). The poignancy of their friendship makes *Of Mice and Men* one of the most unforgettable novels ever written. (The sentence following the quote supports the GAB quote on the importance of connecting with other human beings.)

GLUE. Link sentences. This requires what we call "glue," which refers to connecting words and phrases that unite your paragraphs. As you experiment with these excellent helpers, you will see how much better your writing sounds with these in place. At first, work with your "glue list" close by, and when you link sentences, choose ones that make sense. Eventually, these will roll right into your mind, and you will no longer need to check your list unless looking for more variety. In fact, if you prefer, write your entire essay and then go back and plug in GLUE words and phrases.

GOODBYE. Sum up what you originally promised readers. Restate the thesis in different words to end your essay.

First Impressions

For practice, write your first impression of a

teacher, a cousin, or a friend. This is your topic sentence (the point you will argue):

A first impression springs from one's own eye, seeing physical aspects; one's own ear, hearing words; and one's own history of experiences, feeling and observing and being.

Note: Because our example comes from the fiction work *Jane Eyre*, author Charlotte Bronte can use "I," but in writing essays, you will use 3rd person instead.

We draw an outstanding first-impression example from the renowned novel *Jane Eyre*, as the protagonist describes Mr. Rochester. In doing so, however, her thoughts capture *her own* character: "I had hardly ever seen a handsome youth; never in my life spoken to one. I had a theoretical reverence and homage for beauty; elegance, gallantry, fascination; but had I met those qualities incarnate in masculine shape, I should have known instinctively that they neither had nor could have sympathy with anything in me, and <u>should have shunned them as one would fire, lightning, or anything else that is bright but antipathetic</u>" (130). Bronte depicts in dramatic words how insignificant Jane Eyre feels in the presence of this stranger. Furthermore, the simile (underlined) reflects Jane's reticence on first encountering a man whose appearance has a huge impact on her. Today, one might say she was "blown away."

Therefore, as you work on your first-impression paragraph, what comparison do you want to use? Tell what you think the person would think of you, as Jane Eyre remarks "I should have known instinctively that they neither had nor could have sympathy with anything in me." She sounds certain that this towering figure could not be interested in her. Note how the sentence reveals her lack of confidence; she is naïve, and her reaction to the man makes her inexperience apparent as Bronte describes it well.

Example: Bart Gregson is like a shadow in the forest, hard to see and even harder to catch.

Example: A bit otherworldly in her graceful movements, Lucy Mason is as fluid as a rainbow—a glimpse of primary colors and then poof, she disappears.

Example: On first impression, Emily Simpson is the quintessential California girl—tall and tan and fit and blonde, but on closer inspection, one sees the glint in her eye, the intensity in her voice, and the fierceness in her intelligence. People are never the simple packages they seem to be on an initial meet-and-greet.

Now you try it! This is fun, and you can't go wrong in making observations. Practice using third person (see examples above).

First Person? It's an Essay Outlaw!

Again, we want to underscore that the passage from *Jane Eyre* is in first person because this is a novel, and you are analyzing it in an essay that you are writing. As we mentioned earlier, in formal essays, you don't use first person because that makes your work sound personal, and an objective viewpoint is preferrable. Thus, remember *not* to use personal pronouns: I, my, me, mine, we, us, our, myself, ourselves. Don't insert yourself into the essay but do back up your argument by quoting someone (GAB).

However, when a quote from a book or poem or short story contains first person, leave it in place. You can, however, omit a few words to shorten it, and do so with an ellipsis, which is dot-dot-dot and looks like the end of this sentence: "The man sighed…"

For example, write this kind of topic sentence:
On first sight on the red carpet at the MTV Video Music Awards September 12, 2010, Lady Gaga in her infamous "meat dress" looks bizarre (Mapes). However, her outrageousness draws fans like the sun attracts beach-lovers who cannot get enough of the sparkling yellow brightness.

Here's our point: Even though you are the one who saw her, you eliminate first person in your essay just by using "fans" instead of "I." Take yourself out of it, and the description is acceptable in a formal essay. And, you still convey the message. Also, avoid: "I think it is wrong for Lady Gaga to wear cuts of beef, and music critic Barry-Joe Wildman thinks so, too."

You *can* write: "Even though Wildman thinks ridiculous costumes are inappropriate for self-expression, Lady Gaga fans disagree, saying 'different strokes for different folks.'" As for Lady Gaga herself, she says this is not an anti-meat statement. "It's certainly no disrespect to anyone that's vegan or vegetarian. ...I'm the most judgment-free human being on the Earth. It has many interpretations, but for me...it's [saying], 'If we don't stand up for what we believe in, if we don't fight for our rights, pretty soon we're going to have as much rights as the meat on our bones'" (Mapes).

Rubrics, Oh No!

A rubric spotlights your teacher's expectations. Review this checklist AFTER you've written your essay; otherwise, there's a chance a rubric will weigh down your lighthearted thought processes. Mainly, glean from a rubric a better understanding of exactly which parts of your essay need work. Therefore, look at rubrics as reminders of important aspects of formal writing.

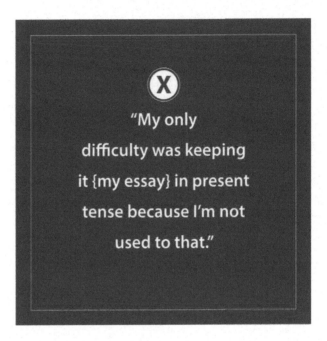

"My only difficulty was keeping it {my essay} in present tense because I'm not used to that."

Don't worry too much about your inability to fathom teacher-talk of "cognitive sentence strategy" and "synthesizing texts." Instead, develop your own yardstick for considering your writing critically:

- Are you arguing your point successfully—or not?

- Are your points clear and step-by-step?

- Does the piece of writing please your audience? If you want to write an article for the school paper, make it entertaining enough to reach peers. In contrast, composing a letter to the editor of your community newspaper requires a more factual, straightforward approach.

- Are you communicating successfully or is your message muddy?
- Does your audience respond the way you hoped they would? If you are trying to move students to join a feed-the-hungry campaign, did people contribute or just yawn?

Love Your Thoughts

Don't forget: You have *your very own fresh way of looking at the world.* Freshman Barton Miller has a lightbulb moment when he hears his teacher assign a paragraph about a person with unique tastes. Here's the prompt: "Some people have an idiosyncratic way of looking at life."

Barton Miller decides to look up the word "idiosyncratic." He thinks he already knows the definition but wants to make sure. (Even longtime writers sometimes discover a definition is a little different from what they thought it was.)

Webster's online says that idiosyncratic means "relating to idiosyncrasy, individual or peculiar." Okay, that's what Barton thought, and the person who came to mind so quickly was his grandfather. So,

Barton writes this paragraph:

One thing great about Granddad is that he does not believe in wasting anything. He never leaves a plate empty. If someone gives him rotten lima beans, he eats them. This man knows what he likes and what he does not like. Specifically, he has this attitude because he remembers the Depression, a time in America when many people did not have enough food to eat. On the other hand, some might say he is just stubborn and likes to prove that everything is edible. One thing for sure, he is never conflicted. He knows what he likes when he likes it.

This boy found a cute way to describe an eccentricity. Barton Miller gives a gut-level description that makes readers smile. Rotten beans? *Okay*. In other words, don't let your mental editor get *too strict*. If you keep throwing away thought after thought for being 'unworthy,' you'll slap down some of the best ideas you have. What comes to mind may not sound sophisticated or slick, but it's definitely not "wrong." Embrace the words flowing from that neuron fountain that is your brain. The more often you do, the better your writing will be.

Writing a good essay is every bit as magical as kicking a field goal in football or winning a trophy for singing. Thus, composing a zinger sentence is exciting! So, go ahead and enjoy the praise—then, ask, "How can I learn to do more of that?" Write sentences that people find relatable. They will love that, and you will, too.

Chapter Nine:
Apply Parking Brakes

Tip for the Day: Even if you feel shaky, putting a strong end on your essay will help diminish that "shrink-wrap" image. Think big. Think vivid. Think dramatic. Leave your reader wanting more.

As you reach your destination, brake gently. Write a GOODBYE conclusion that puts the car in the garage, all snuggled in, locked, and done for the day but also makes your reader want to take one last peek underneath the hood.

Here are ways to give your conclusion some "pop."

- **Leave the reader on a high note.** In your

essay conclusion, simply restate emphatically what you first set out to prove. Your message should ring in readers' ears. Mark Twain ends *Adventures of Huckleberry Finn* by noting how hard it was to "make a book" and then adding "But I reckon I got to light out for the Territory ahead of the rest, because Aunt Sally she's going to adopt me and sivilize (*sic*) me and I can't stand it. I been there before. THE END. YOURS TRULY. HUCK FINN" (Twain 263). After getting to know Huck, the reader grins, thinking that this conclusion puts a perfect period on an enchanting journey.

- **End your essay with one last assertion.** Point out one last time *why you think what you do* about the topic. Author Emily Bronte, in her novel *Wuthering Heights*, ended the story with this comment made in a graveyard: "I...watched the moths fluttering among the heath and hare-bells; listened to the soft wind breathing through the grass; and wondered how anyone could ever imagine unquiet slumbers for the sleepers in that quiet earth" (308).

- **Remind readers of the "evidence"** you presented to support your argument. An appropriate closing sentence for an essay on

Anne Frank's memorable *The Diary of a Young Girl* might be this: *Readers are moved to see a girl endure heartbreak yet still retain a hopeful spirit, and what carries the message over the finish line is Frank's effective use of rhetorical appeals.*

The conclusion can be incredibly powerful. End with a bang. Write a "GOODBYE" that leaves readers wishing they could read more.

For a killer conclusion to an essay:

- Mention the main points you want readers to keep in mind. Takeaways!

- Say one last time what you hope readers got from reading the essay.

- Include a last bit of encouragement for readers to take action.

- Write a final "summation" that sounds emphatic.

- Remind readers of the "promise" you made.

The easiest way to end on a high note is to restate in different words what you set out originally to prove. Shakespeare's last lines of the tragedy *Romeo and Juliet* resonate perfectly when he writes, "For never was a story of more woe/Than this of Juliet and her Romeo" (243 Shakespeare). *Way to go, Will!*

Chapter Ten:
Follow Your Checklist

Tip for the Day: Grow confidence by referring to your checklist. Never hurts to take a glance at the requirements and make sure you checked all the boxes. Now that you're feeling more comfortable with classroom learning, ask your teacher to confirm that you're on the right track. She can glance over your essay and quickly tell you if something is still missing.

Basic tips. These can keep you from wrecking your brand-new writer wheels. Keep a reference list nearby so you can double-check these items until you internalize them.

- I got rid of all contractions.

- I wrote in present tense.
- I included TAG.
- I came up with a zinger GRAB sentence.
- For GAB, I pulled an appropriate quote from a book I am reading. (Appropriate means that it supports what you set out to prove, not just a quote that you happen to like.)
- I was careful to weave my GAB quote into a sentence, so it didn't stick out.
- I explained why I included this GAB quote.
- I used GLUE.
- I made my GOODBYE memorable.

That's your checklist. Keep it handy.

Waxing Your Vehicle

Want to make your essay extra shiny? Include words that are different from the ones you use over and over. Vibrant vocabulary helps. Dip into synonyms.

Think of what you would you say to someone about a cool YouTube video you just finished watching. You would be enthusiastic: "Man, you have to watch this one—it's hilarious! You'll laugh till you cry." Similarly, you can connect with your topic so completely that ideas bubble up and supply high-energy words for your essays.

Watch for Landmines

Most importantly, tamp down the hailstorm of negativity that nags you while you're writing. Identify that brain reel that repeats creepy naysaying: "I'm the worst writer in class," or "our teacher thinks just two kids write good essays and the rest of us, not so much," or "I'm never going to be a good writer because my siblings weren't."

Faulty assumptions won't help. Shake them off. Decide that every time one of those bad boys tries to clamp down on your brain, you're going to banish it. No longer will you buy into the idea that you are "less than" in any area of life. Toss all troublemakers.

Loosen up Before You Write

Take a short walk. Put on workout clothes or just go with what you're wearing. Walk around the block a time or two and immerse yourself in nature. Let the structure of a lush bougainvillea bush amaze you. Notice a butterfly flitting by in all its elegance. Think about our big world and how you are one small *but important* element in it. There is beauty in your thoughts, and now you're going back home to write them down.

If depressing news disturbs you, turn off the TV or turn away from your smart phone. Declare news-free days. Be like Scarlett O'Hara in *Gone with the Wind* and say, "I'll think about that tomorrow."

Do a ten-minute vent. Ask a friend or relative to listen and tell that person you just want to say what's on your mind, no feedback needed. After you finish, breathe deeply and wiggle your head around to prep your mind for performing great tricks.

Make a list of six "items" for the day, and on it, put: "Take a walk. Do a ten-minute vent." Okay, check off those two. Silly as it sounds, I do this all the time—always have, and it jumpstarts me by proving that yes, I actually do get things done.

Decide what's toughest on your list and tackle that first. Then, go to the others. If you have to move things to your "Tomorrow" list, don't stew about it. Be good to yourself. Stop comparing. A zillion times in my life, I've beaten myself up about poor organizational skills, and guess what? They didn't get better, but I finally asked people to help me. Today, I can stand and marvel at someone who organizes a closet or room, as if there were nothing to it. Watching my friends Jenny Amahan and Connie Gonzales redo my wickedly out-of-control closets, I realized that their skills as organizers came as naturally as mine in writing 100 pages.

There is the lesson! People are good at different things. Doesn't mean we stop working on challenges, but some skills *really are* almost impossible for certain people. Quit telling yourself that you would be a terrific person if only you were good at cooking or organizing or singing. That is ridiculous, and you know it. Weaknesses just prove we are human.

Besides, who likes someone who is great at everything? That kind of person scares us. In fact, the only "perfect" ones we do enjoy are those who help us with our weaknesses. So, if you are Mr. or Ms.

Perfect, remember that you won't be Prom King or Queen forever, so get down off that pedestal and meet a few who are less lordly. They're pretty adorable, too.

Another calming practice is to recall kudos that people have given you over the years. It feels good. When you're listing deficits, take time to turn to positive thoughts, too, and enjoy the hugs.

Praise your own strengths. Maybe you're the kind of friend who is so inclusive that no one ever feels left out when you're around. That's a great trait! What if you're the guy in the neighborhood who always comes running when an elderly neighbor falls? How kind! There are many standout characteristics *in you* just waiting to be noticed. Problem is, most of us focus on negatives: "My hair is too thin. I'm too outspoken. My essay ideas are boring. I'll never be able to make money writing. I don't like that my eyes slant downward…"

Somewhere in our culture, someone is always going to whisper that you have value only if you're brilliant and beautiful and effervescent. Guess what? It's a lie. So, don't listen. There is value and beauty in every person, even those who struggle to learn, have average looks, and loathe speaking in public. *Loving who you are* is one thing you can do to accentuate your natural beauty and your innate intelligence and, while you're at it, make your essays hip-hip-hooray-crazy-world successes.

People who glow with confidence stand out. They are compelling to know. The more often you give voice to your wonderful ideas, the more often you will get the attention you so richly deserve. (Also keep in mind a basic rule of human interactions and also a best-kept secret: The people around you mainly want to know what you think *about them*.)

What you're writing can influence those who read your ideas. Your writing can have huge consequences. For that to happen, though, you must fashion your message to communicate well with *your audience*. Know your readers.

Follow the guidepost inside you that asks: What is the need in the heart and soul of my reader? Imagine the impact of your words, from entertainment to world-changing. Then you really "get" how critical it is to maximize your word power and use it effectively and beneficially. Believe it or not, your words can end up improving humankind, and wouldn't that be wonderful? You can be an almost-perfect driver of the "mind wheels" at your disposal—the writer who reaches a destination skillfully and articulates a mission clearly and thus changes minds and hearts.

For very good reasons, we quote leaders like JFK

and FDR and MLK and others, and often the "voice" behind those stunning speakers was a speechwriter whose name you do not know. However, many powerful messages have made a difference in this magnificent country. That alone should show you the importance of perfecting language so that your communications are concise, clear, correct, and catchy. You may wind up speechwriter for a President, or the actual *President*—and decide to be that rare, elected official who writes his own stuff.

Avoid Potholes on the Road to Great Essays

Basic tips can keep any high school essay writer from wrecking. Keep a list of these nearby so you can double-check them until you internalize them.

What's the most typical essay mess-up? The gnarly run-on sentence is one trap. Close behind is the fragment. You, an up-and-coming essayist, will avoid both bumps and do quick fixes on them.

Run-ons and fragments stall communication because readers have to stop and try to figure them out. Also, when your teacher reviews your essay, run-ons and fragments jump out like fire-spewing dragons. In other words, these are just wrong for formal writing. Go ahead and put them in posts, emails, and text messages, but edit them out of all essays you write. Keep telling yourself that writing essays *isn't* texting. Instead of dashing out a fast message, you are *developing* thoughts on paper.

Quick Fixes

Try your skills. In the below practice, mark "F" if it's a fragment, and mark "R" if it's a run-on sentence. Then, turn the sentence into a real one. A run-on becomes two sentences, or a sentence with a semi-colon, or a sentence with a connecting word (and, but, etc.). A fragment needs more words to make it a complete thought.

- The students got wet waiting at the bus stop it was a rainy day.
- Should have worn raincoats.
- The students went to school with wet hair sometimes that happens.
- Congress held hearings on the COVID pandemic did that help, though?
- No one other than criminals liked wearing masks it made some people feel breathless.
- Pandemic rules were suggested whatever those rules were, people did not always follow them.
- Teens did not want to give their grandparents COVID that was a scary thought.
- Six boys had lunch together at Spaghetti Diner five tested positive for COVID.

- Must be very contagious.
- Many symptoms on the list.

Takeaways

Use the Autopilot Essay when you're on a tight schedule; you have to get to debate practice at 5:00, dinner at 6:30, and homework, 7:30. However, when you want to ENLARGE ON your essay writing, turn to PART II and try to get your arms around those upper-level ideas and terms. That's where you go after you've mastered the basics and want to train for the Grand Prix of essay driving, which will be college or the corporate world or anyplace that requires more complex writing.

You can improve on your:

- Writing quality
- Organizing of thoughts
- Word choice
- Sentence structure variety
- Amount of writing output
- Ability to write for different kinds of audiences instead of one-size-fits-all
- Ability to use evidence quotes effectively
- Goal-setting, drafting, evaluating, revising, and editing
- Detail, examples, and evidence that support

your main idea

- Analysis of reading and writing

Challenge Yourself

Here's an easy ask. Select a current event online and write an article on it. Explain what is happening, who is doing it, when, why, and where (the famous "5 Ws" that are basics of journalistic writing).

Let's say, for this challenge, that you will:

Argue that Morton Community Park should not be reserved for kids' birthday parties. Write three paragraphs.

Points you can include:

- Lowman Brag, a local sports legend who learned basketball as a kid shooting hoops at Morton Park, thinks reserving the park is a bad idea because it limits people who can make use of the facilities on those days. Mr. Brag plans to speak before City Council. "I do not think it is fair for parents to reserve the park for birthday parties since city parks are meant to provide free entertainment for one and all," said Lowman Brag.

- Mandy McGuire, mother of three, is in favor of reserving the park because she does so every time one of her children has a birthday. "I don't think it hurts to set off

a part of the park for a birthday party,"
says McGuire. "There are trails and
athletic fields open and available."

- City Council member Hardy Lane says,
  "We get lots of complaints about the fact
  that birthday parties take up all the swings
  and play equipment for a slot of three
  hours on a Saturday or Sunday. For
  parents who work, this is their only day to
  take their kids to the park."

- Ten-year-old Adam North says, "We like
  to go there to hang out, but if there's a
  birthday party going on, some adult
  usually sends us away."

In a three-paragraph essay, argue that it is wrong
to reserve a park for birthday parties. Back it up with
at least two quotes. Since you are arguing "against,"
you also must give the other side's opinion. Word the
contrarian viewpoint this way: "Others say that
reserving the park allows kids a special place to have a
party." OR this way: "On the other hand, some
people praise the notion of having a park serve both
individual and group purposes." After you give your
basic argument, give the counter argument. This
means presenting how the other side feels about this
issue, which is key to an essay that argues a point, also
known as an "argumentative essay."

GRAB: Your intro paragraph should have a good hook and a topic sentence that tells the reader what you will argue.

GAB: Include at least two quotes from the ones we provided. After you use a quote, don't forget to explain how it backs up your topic sentence and why it matters.

GLUE: Make sure your sentences connect with glue.

GOODBYE: Write final sentences that sum up your argument.

Check It Out

- Proofread for mistakes.

- Substitute overused words with synonyms.

- Delete clichés. Substitute fresher words that aren't "tired" from overuse.

- Make sure your writing leads but does not mislead.

- Take out information that gets off track and does not apply to the topic.

- Use specifics. Instead of saying "park," specify "Morton Park." Instead of saying the boy eats cereal daily, say that he likes Cheerios for breakfast. Instead of saying the woman sits at Morton Park with her laptop, tell readers it's an Apple laptop.

- Insert GAB (evidence quotes) into place so that these don't stick out oddly. You must thread the quote into a sentence.

How Many Words Can a Word-Stocker Shop?

You are sitting down to write a persuasive essay. Your topic sentence is: *Some people get on everyone's nerves, but it is always better to get to know someone rather than jumping on the shaming bandwagon.*

Now, use a GAB quote to back up your point (see the underlined part).

"Fashion your message to communicate well with your audience."

Some people get on everyone's nerves, but it is always better to get to know someone rather than jumping on the shaming bandwagon. For example, the character Boo Radley in the novel *To Kill a Mockingbird*, by Harper Lee, scares the children Scout and Jem because they think he is spooky. However, as their relationship with him changes, both kids accept his differences and discover that Boo is just a lonely man. The children's father, Atticus Finch, tells them "You never really understand a person until you consider things from his point of view, until you climb into his skin and walk around in it" (33). Thus, the point is that first impressions are often wrong, and that means people should look deeper and find things they have in common with an individual they do not understand.

See how GLUE connects: for example, however, thus.

Now, check out this excerpt from *Jane Eyre* to see how author Charlotte Bronte uses GLUE in 1874: "Meantime, Mr. Rochester had again summoned the ladies round him, and was selecting certain of their number...{for} his party. 'Miss Ingram is mine, of course,' said he: afterwards he named the two Misses Eshton, and Mrs. Dent. He looked at me: I happened to be near him, as I had been fastening...Mrs. Dent's bracelet, which had got loose" (Bronte 207).

Transitions, as GLUE, are underlined.

Example: "I think, <u>moreover...</u>" (Bronte 393).

Also of interest is Bronte's frequent use of metaphors: "...Nature was not to him that treasury of delight..." This illustrates how authorial style often is a natural outgrowth of a person's writing. In 1874, no one was teaching Charlotte Bronte to use figurative language; by following her instinctive way with words, she stirred emotion in audiences.

Unravel That/Which

If you want to impress true masters of English (and look great on your college essays), learn how to use "that/which" correctly. In today's dwindling grammar climate, choosing "that" or "which" for a sentence often turns out to be just a whatever-feels-good kind of thing. Why? Most writers aren't sure what's right. (Truthfully, I have known English professors who use "that/which" incorrectly.)

Admittedly, your essay will not run off into a ditch just because you slip up, but why not learn how to use "that" and "which"? It comes down to a simple rule of necessity; either the sentence really, truly NEEDS the clause of concern—or it does *not* need it because the clause just adds description.

For example, in the following sentence, the clause *is necessary*. Otherwise, no one would know which winning beagle the judge is choosing. The clause is essential, defining, necessary; you NEED it! *For winner of the beagle show, Mrs. Persnickety chose the beagle that has freckles and a beanie hat.* OR: For winner of the dog show, Mrs. Persnickety chose the beagle, which has freckles and a beanie hat.

In the second sentence, if you omit the clause "which has freckles and a beanie hat," the reader does not know which beagle was winner of the beagle show. That tells you that the clause is NECESSARY and needs a "that." (Necessary is also called *restrictive* and *essential* and *defining*.) It's a must to include the descriptive clause "that has freckles and a beanie hat."

Conversely, in the following, it is okay to use "which" because the clause is not 100% necessary: Shih-tzus, which are cuddly, cute dogs, have won the lap-dog contest forty times in past years. The clause "which are cuddly, cute dogs" is just *extra information* that adds to the sentence but *is not* critical to its meaning, the point of which is to designate the breed that has won the lap-dog contest forty times.

If this seems like a whopper explanation for a small rule, you're right—it is. But writers make this mistake often, and editors of books miss it and let it fly by. That's why it's so easy to find a that/which error in published books. Really, if you really want to be a topnotch grammarian, why not just KNOW what's correct and follow the rule on that/which? Then you don't have to rely on a book editor who may (or may not) know how to use that/which. I've explained this to some smart people who wanted to know, but I just get glazed-over eyes. See if you get it.

- Think of a clause that you *need* as DEFINING and ESSENTIAL and in need of the word "THAT."

- Think of a clause that you can toss away as NONDEFINING and NONESSENTIAL and requiring the word "WHICH."

- In other words, any clause leading with the word "which" has to be as disposable as a broken balloon. **Which = toss it. That = keep it. Simple deal.**

Here are several examples:

An individual can learn the grammar rule two ways: first, by memorization, which is easier; second, by imitation, which is clumsier. NOTE that the words set off by "which" are discardable, fluff. You can get rid of them, and no one cares.

Finding a political party that is not spinning out of control is a tough task.

Now, in the above, NOTE that without pointing out the particular party you mean—*the one spinning out of control*—the sentence means nothing. So, the clause is essential.

Miss Merryman's favorite exercise class is Pilates, which is offered three times a week (clause is nonessential here).

Miss Merryman takes the exercise class that is offered three times a week (here, the clause has the only concrete information, and that makes it necessary).

Another way to solve your "that/which" conundrum is recalling that you use a comma to set off a "which" clause, but you don't use one to set off a "that" clause. Typically, a comma indicates "here's some extra info so you can take it or leave it."

What would you choose in the following example?

- *Of Mr. Manus's three athletic sons, he points out <u>the one that is participating in the Olympics in water polo.</u>* NECESSARY CLAUSE

- *Of Mr. Manus's three athletic sons, he points out <u>the one who is participating in the Olympics.</u>* NECESSARY CLAUSE

- *Of Mr. Manus's three athletic sons, he points out the one, which is participating in the Olympics in water polo. (Wrong! Never, ever use "which" to refer to a person.)*

The correct ones are number one and two because the clause is needed. In the third one, if you toss out "which is participating…," you have a nonsensical message. The one? *What about* the one? Again, the clause is essential, important, and needed.

PART II:
The Cruise-Control Essay

For those of you who want to get published, accept that writing requires perseverance. You can't be a quitter. You never, ever give up. You're a writer, and that means you just keep writing and writing. Really, the Cruise-Control Essay, in effect, is your show car. Going beyond the basics of the Autopilot Essay, this writing "vehicle" shines, and so do you. (For this book, our quickie 30-minute Autopilot Essay comes in handy for those writers who just want to learn the basics.)

Writing is infinitely enjoyable if you can accept that it can be hard work: brainstorming, planning, revision, etc. The happy endeavor, though, makes it worth every minute. Most writers don't get rich or famous (maybe notorious), but most really do love their profession. Writers are typically in the shadows, not the spotlight, and the longer they stay there, the more comfortable they are with being the people behind the showboats.

Chapter Eleven:
Live Large in Five Paragraphs

Tip for the Day: Connect to what you are doing. You are part of a demographic sometimes called "people of purpose." That just means your brain checks out fast if something doesn't serve you or your interests. HOWEVER! The essay topic has no problem with being unliked. The "why" is the most important part of whatever you write. So, when you are assigned the gift of a "free-write" or "open topic" essay, write on something you're passionate about and lend your special voice to it.

Hey, brainiac. Let your onboard computer—your brain—tick off elements you want to include in your essay. GRAB, GAB, GLUE, GOODBYE. Once you have those squared away, add embellishments, and move your essay into high gear.

Try the pattern (p.151) for writing a five-paragraph essay. After using essay organizers in the past, remember that a rigid, lockstep essay is what you DON'T WANT. Still, though, school essays need a "topic sentence," which we call GRAB, and the ever-popular "evidence," which we call GAB, as well as the GLUE, that wonderful essential that adds cohesion, not to mention the GOODBYE, which is your conclusion.

Each body paragraph deals with one topic, the same one you put in your paragraph's topic sentence. Everything in your paragraph must refer back to that topic. You can't switch gears and suddenly discuss something else. (If you do, you'll have to cut it later.) When you are ready to talk about something else that applies to your thesis sentence, start a new paragraph and write on and on for the next part of your essay.

A new idea? Again, you move on to the next paragraph. Write a topic sentence that is straightforward and focused and supports the overall thesis sentence you advanced in your intro. Follow that topic sentence like a private investigator, and you'll stay on track. Do not let it out of your surveillance eye.

148

After you have written an introductory paragraph (GRAB), three body paragraphs (GAB), and the conclusion (GOODBYE), edit so that you can hit "done" by the deadline, as your model zips into place at the front of the pack. Check to see that you have inserted enough GLUE words and phrases (transitions) for maximum flow. Read the essay out loud and listen. If it sounds like it all wraps together as harmoniously as a BLTA sandwich, then you are done ("A" is for avocado, by the way).

Douse Those Doubts

Many students get nervous when writing "serious" essays, and that makes it doubly important to get past your reluctance to "bother" a teacher. Most of the time, teens do not understand how eager teachers are to foster success. A student can really profit from hearing a teacher clarify an assignment. Ask and you will be helped.

Experienced teachers say that one of the biggest mistakes their students make is failing to speak up when an assignment confuses them. Often a kid will just sink lower because it feels awful to miss a key point the teacher is making. Plus, you look around the classroom, and no one else has a "what the heck?" expression. English teacher Melissa Mead points out, "I can promise you there are others who don't get it

> **Follow that topic sentence like a private investigator, and you'll stay on track.**

either, so be sure to reach out."

Of course, reticence makes it hard to hold up your hand in class, but when you don't, the hole you dig gets deeper. As the teacher builds on a point that you never understood in the first place, you dim your own prospects of delivering. Think of it this way: It's okay to be confused, but it's not okay to *stay* confused. Work hard to break down barriers that have you convinced that asking questions will (a) make you sound dumb (b) make the teacher angry, or

(c) make classmates stare at you. Just word your question respectfully, and other kids will be thankful, as in "whew, I was hoping someone would ask that…"

However, don't take 10 minutes to ask a 30-second question. *This is no time for your labradoodle story.* As an example, when your teacher gives instructions for writing an essay based on a syllogism, feel free to ask, "what's a 'syllogism'?" Then the teacher defines the term, and you're no longer confused.

Time for Liftoff!

If you prefer to have a *blueprint for success*, try the pattern below for writing a five-paragraph essay.

PATTERN: Here's your easy-to-follow "setup" for essay success:

<u>**Introductory Paragraph**</u> (3-4 sentences)

GRAB (thesis sentence)—Introduce what you're writing about or arguing. This one is also called a thesis sentence because it's an "umbrella" for the whole five-paragraph essay. Everything falls under the GRAB. Say HOW you plan to prove your claim and the source of quotes you will use to support that claim.

GOODBYE—Sum up introductory thoughts.

<u>**Body Paragraph 1**</u> (4-5 sentences)

GRAB—Write a straightforward topic sentence

that lays out the main idea for this paragraph. It must support the claim in the intro.

GAB (Evidence 1)—Pull a quote from the text, and let it ride shotgun with your main idea. The quote must have content that connects to this paragraph's topic sentence.

GLUE—Using transition "glue" words, link your claim and quote. In two or three sentences, explain how your GAB quote supports your claim.

GOODBYE—Sum up your paragraph thoughts.

Body Paragraph 2 (4-5 sentences)

GRAB—State another main idea that supports the claim from your intro paragraph.

GAB (Evidence 2)—Pull a second quote to ride shotgun with your main idea.

GLUE—Connect your claim and quote with glue. Explain how your GAB quote backs up your main idea.

GOODBYE—Sum up thoughts from this paragraph.

Body Paragraph 3 (4-5 sentences)

GRAB—In a solid topic statement, present your third main idea that supports the claim from your intro paragraph.

GAB (Evidence 3)—Pull another text quote to support your main idea.

GLUE—Connect your claim and quote with

adhesive. Explain how your GAB quote backs up your main idea.

GOODBYE—Sum up the thoughts in this paragraph.

Concluding Paragraph (2-3 sentences)

GRAB—Restate your original thesis sentence in different words. Paraphrase.

GOODBYE—Sum up thoughts. Point to the evidence you gave in paragraphs two, three, and four. Close on a clear, emphatic note.

Now Look What You've Done

Keeping in mind what you've learned about essays, review these sentences a student attending an arts school wrote for her seminar class. The student writer, though an artist herself, keeps personal opinions out of the essay and seeks solely to prove her thesis statement. (Here, we include a short excerpt.)

Activist Art: The Fight for the Preservation of Culture and Virtue

Every culture gives rise to art organically; in fact, *culture simply does not exist without art*. Because of its essentiality, then, art fuels sociocultural development, progression, and change, as a bold change-maker. In particular, current societal issues have spawned a reactionary art genre called "activist art."

The activist art movement allows art makers to

express perspectives in efforts to spark societal change. One notable example of activism art is the Black Arts Movement that emerged during the civil rights era and peaked after the assassination of Dr. Martin Luther King, Jr. No doubt, King's passionate speeches paved the way for black voices in media via activism art. As Dr. King noted, "Nonviolent direct action seeks to create such a crisis and foster such a tension that a community which has constantly refused to negotiate is forced to confront the issue. It seeks so to dramatize the issue that it can no longer be ignored" ("Letter from Birmingham Jail").

Americans tend to agree that *all* political art—controversial or not, activist or not—can be part of modern media alongside traditional news as long as political art does not encourage illegal or destructive acts. At its best, provocative art can serve as a trailblazer in sociocultural change. By creating advocates for silenced persons, such movements shape modern societies. The civil rights era, for example, ushered in activism art that gave black communities hope, leaders, and media connections (Milbrandt). Art also helped desegregate America. In effect, the Black Arts Movement (BAM) revealed the resilience of black communities by establishing a black presence in modern culture. BAM works symbolize the growth in appreciation of once-muzzled voices. Thus, activist art, paired with expressions of dissatisfaction, can achieve tangible change.

Even so, however, the scope of artist visibility remains narrow because large art movements often ignore the oppressed. All too often, the main advocates of reactionary art movements fail to represent the masses they reflect. However ironic it is, prejudice sneaks into the mix. Furthermore, primary advocates and the media shun some advocates by branding them too radical or not radical enough. Therefore, when making policy changes regarding activism art, leaders seem immune to the needs of the "every man."

Art restrictions, of course, are inevitably arbitrary and subjective; imposing rules evokes unjust censorship. This is why it is far better to present rather than restrict messaged art. Again, activism art, in particular, is designed to create discomfort and let individuals react. However, shock value as the distinguishing factor in activist art could lead to a dark future for "respectable" activist art. In addition, ethically speaking, even the act of excluding political art detracts from art's purpose. Also coming to bear are antiquated legal precedents that dictate current legislation on protection of provocative art works.

Certainly, culture without art is unimaginable.

The symbols, the images, the colors, the textures—all are inherently parts of the soundtracks of lives: the mirrors of agonies and ecstasies. Art and pathos, wildflowers and bonfires are reasons to exist.

Note: This student's teacher suggests adding some short sentences for variety. Overall, though, the essay is presented thoughtfully in both ideas and word choices.

Read. Read. Read.

Remember, if you want to be a better singer, listen to plenty of music and practice your vocals. The same goes for writing. If you want to be a better writer, incorporate more reading into your life, and, of course, write more.

Start with 30 minutes of reading per day, and it won't take long to become a legit *logophile*, or "lover of words." Not only will your vocabulary grow, but you will relieve anxiety just by increasing your daily reading and writing. Scientific fact!

Chapter Twelve:
Do 2nd and 3rd Prewrites

Tip for the Day: After assessing your essay prewrite, your English teacher makes these suggestions: Improve your topic sentence and use stronger evidence quotes. Respond to both ideas for making your essay better.

Edit. Now that you know how to use GRAB, GAB, GLUE, GOODBYE, you can put the "muscle" in your muscle car. Move into high gear. Knowing the four-G basics greases your wheels, allowing smooth traction for a finish in less than 30 minutes.

Don't overthink ideas. Just go for it, putting

down exactly what comes to your mind about the topic. Today. No edits. Focus on flow. Even if you find yourself making errors, like contractions, move on. You'll have time to shine your vehicle later.

If you choose to use the five-paragraph skeleton, stay flexible. Clinging too closely to any format can *stifle creativity*. If you rely too much on getting things in the right places, you tend to forget what you're doing and deliver limp sentences.

Stick to delivering all the parts: the GRAB topic sentence, the ever-popular evidence quote GAB, GLUE for cohesion, and a GOODBYE wrap-up. It is a package, and omitting elements is as big a mistake as a grocery delivery lacking water, bread, and (of course) cookies.

You and Will Shakespeare

One day after your class finishes reading Shakespeare's *Hamlet*, your teacher asks you to write on the *causal relationship* between two important quotes from the play: One is "The time is out of joint. O cursed spite! That ever I was born to set it right," and the other is "to be or not to be, that is the question." Honestly, this assignment scares you. Sounds hard, and that "old language" of Shakespearean works is daunting. Then you remember: *wait, I'm a good writer. I've got this.*

After all, the plot, which includes ghosts and murders, is simple. Most important is that Hamlet is an indecisive young man who is furious because his uncle killed his father (the king) and then married Hamlet's mother. The kingdom is in chaos, obviously, and Hamlet is sad, angry, and unsure how to exact payback. In the words "the time is out of joint," he is saying in ancient lingo that he wishes the murder hadn't happened—it's bad timing. In the line "O cursed spite! That ever I was born to set it right," he is mad that he is the one stuck with the job of fixing family dynamics. It's not his thing. Unfortunately, he is the guy who always has trouble making up his mind and sorting out this crisis requires someone who can act decisively.

Hamlet gets so distraught (bent out of shape) that he even wonders if death might be better than being forced to act as kingdom cleanup man. For that pivotal moment, Shakespeare gives Hamlet the famous line that will be quoted over the centuries: "to be or not to be." This is part of an eloquent rant that essentially says, "Do I really want to seek justice for my father's murder by killing my mother's new husband?" You, the reader, think: "Wow, no wonder they call this a tragedy."

As for the causality aspect of the essay, a reader can see that the line "to be or not to be" *does cause* the content of the line "O cursed spite!" If Hamlet were not maximally indecisive, he would act without overthinking the decision. Hence, when your teacher asks for a causal relationship, you can see one. So, for an A+ essay:

- You're going to prove the causality.
- You're going to use quotes from the play.
- You will cite each spot where a quote appears and put page-number citations in parentheses.
- Start with a catchy beginning that will engage readers who may not want to read this essay because they think Shakespeare is stuffy and difficult.

Basically, your teacher tells the class not to feel confined to any particular format, but including quotes is a must. Imagine a royal family squabble gone bad, and write.

Of course, you want to capture Hamlet's conflicted mental state concerning the no-win situation (1.5. 210-211). You're showing that the moment has a causal relationship with another defining moment in the play, and that is the famous "to be or not to be" soliloquy. That comes as an

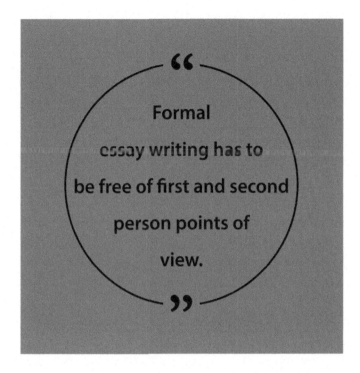

Formal essay writing has to be free of first and second person points of view.

organic extension of his original discontent, in which Hamlet ponders whether life or death is the better option of the two, since he is unable to choose a course of action (3.1.64). Begin by plopping thoughts on paper. Then spend 15 minutes reading an article online or a few pages from a nonfiction book. The point is to examine a nonfiction point of view (POV) and study how that writer persuades.

Next, you write. After you finish your first draft, let it go "cold." This means leave it alone overnight or even for a day or two. Then, the next time you meet with that essay, read it, and you'll see how the weak parts jump out at you and beg to be deleted.

Don't skip this "ice-bucket" step. Second and third looks at an essay help you finetune your message and maximize your good parts. However, anytime a simile, metaphor, or unique vocabulary word stops you, don't toss it out *just because it sounds unfamiliar.*

Never eliminate a unique thought without a good reason. Otherwise, you'll slice out the best and brightest of your sentences. Be a tough critic, but do not snuff out that candle of brilliance. If you're not sure if something quirky actually works, run it past a teacher or parent or friend, and ask for an honest opinion.

Dissect This Essay

This "Hamlet" essay, shortened to fit here as an example, shows how one student writes on Hamlet's set of "Royals." (By the way, Shakespeare's characters often speak in what is called a "soliloquy." This is a character thinking out loud when alone.)

Hamlet: King of Indecisiveness

Bodies pile up. Ghosts give orders. People fight. However, in William Shakespeare's play *Hamlet*, what stands out most is that Hamlet personifies a universal malaise sometimes referred to as "the human condition." In the first defining moment of significance, the lines "The time is out of joint. O cursed spite/ That ever I was born to set it right" perfectly capture Hamlet's conflicted mental state as he confronts a no-win situation (1.5.210-211). This moment has a causal relationship with another defining moment in the play—his famous "to be or not to be" soliloquy, which evolves from the discontent in which Hamlet ponders life versus death (3.1.64). By this point, Hamlet leans toward choosing life but also knows that he still has to avenge his father's death. These defining moments are wildly successful characterizations, as Shakespeare finds ideal phrases to express life-altering points of no return.

At the play's outset, Shakespeare acquaints readers with Hamlet's chaotic emotions concerning his father's death, his mother's hasty marriage, and his mixed feelings toward his love Ophelia. Hamlet portrays the dominant theme of madness that is a strong narrative thread. He could be a philosopher or a madman; however, his anger seems justified, considering his family's dysfunction.

Furthermore, Hamlet verbally abuses his girlfriend Ophelia by suggesting "get thee to a nunnery," which is his way of saying he is done with her (3.1.131). He boasts, "I am very proud, revengeful, ambitious, with more offenses at my beck than I have thoughts... We are errant knaves; believe none of us" (3.1.134-140). Then he promises a plague for a wedding gift if she marries. And if that is not demeaning enough, Hamlet tells her to "marry a fool, for wise men know well enough what monsters you make of them" (3.1.150-151). Ophelia decides the nunnery is sounding better all the time.

Hamlet sees fate's double-edged sword. The causal relationship between "cursed spite" and the subsequent "to be/not to be" is that the reader is drawn into the eroding brain of Hamlet, which is a frightening place to be (3.1.64). Gone is the initial impression that Hamlet is just reluctant to act. What he actually needs is mental health intervention. Then again, maybe he is just a melodramatic man especially fond of hyperbole.

Hamlet, the over-thinker, postpones getting justice for his father. He must kill Claudius but waiting for proof sends Hamlet over the edge. The ending, when Claudius also plans death for Hamlet, assures the reader that Hamlet will kill or be killed. The foreshadowing of misfortunes cannot be overturned.

At any rate, when Hamlet presents his gloomy speech about life or death, the reader wonders if this grim man should be left to pick his poison. As he continues to weigh death versus life, the reader wants to scream, "Man, just make a decision."

On the other hand, how can he assess his options with no notion of the afterlife? Furthermore, Hamlet is still angry that he got the assignment, aka "born to set it right," and his extreme self-pity grates on reader's nerves. He hates that "conscience does make cowards of us all," meaning that Hamlet thinks suicide is sinful (3.1.91). Being warned to avenge his father's death is disconcerting when a ghost hints that old King Hamlet is not going to rest in heaven until someone kills Claudius.

Hamlet still vacillates, complaining that villainous Claudius ruined everything; it is his fault Hamlet is estranged from his mother, and it is his fault Hamlet has no father. Hamlet's conflicted state is his tragic flaw, which is evident when he says, "O cursed spite/That ever I was born to set it right" (1.5.210-211). He worries that seeking revenge will only highlight his failures as a hero.

Finally, assessing two causal epiphanies in *Hamlet*, the reader sees Hamlet fulfill his destiny, but most of the characters die, anyway. The two turning points' causal links prove that Hamlet endures the "not to be" aspect of his famed soliloquy, but "to be" is no longer in play. Hence, Hamlet survives the human condition but loses the war.

Think. Review. Edit.

When you finish your own Hamlet essay, study your work with a critical eye. Make sure you have TAG and GRAB-GAB-GLUE-GOODBYE in place. Ensure, too, that nothing has crept into your work that doesn't belong there. *Examples:* "I'm going to tell you about how Hamlet's indecision caused trouble in his kingdom." Avoid that kind of start or "my name is" or "I'm going to tell you about Hamlet" or even "my opinion is."

Grown-up essay writing has to be smarter, crisper, and free of first and second person points of view. To refresh your memory, first person is "I, me, our, we" and second person is "you and your." (Save those for narratives, memoirs, short stories, and novels.)

Also, review your essay for present tense.

Example: Hamlet <u>had</u> a way of postponing decisions, but this <u>was</u> a character trait the audience kind of <u>enjoyed</u> because it <u>foreshadowed</u> trouble. It should say: Hamlet <u>has</u> a way of postponing decisions, but this <u>is</u> a character trait the audience kind of <u>enjoys</u> because it <u>foreshadows</u> trouble.

In the first example, the words "had," "was," "enjoyed," and "foreshadowed" are all in past tense—not correct in formal essays. In the second example, though, the words "has," "is," "enjoy," and "foreshadows" are in present tense, which is perfect for a formal essay. This is easy to get wrong because most people story-tell in past tense—it's a habit.

One last step: use active voice, not passive. **Pin this example on your bulletin board.**

- The dog bites the boy. (Active voice so yes, this one is right!)

- The boy was bitten by the dog. (Passive voice so no, this one is wrong.)

- Hamlet finally makes a decision. (Active voice)

- Hamlet was haunted by the need to make a decision. (Passive voice)

Keep in mind that you're trotting out something no other writer has, no matter how great his talent; that is your *fresh way of looking at the world. Your thoughts. Your words. Your voice.*

Chapter Thirteen:
Use Rhetorical Appeals

Tip for the Day: Is your overdrive mode overwhelming you?
Some kids find that being back in regular classrooms is
jumpstarting them, all right, but to an exhausting degree. So,
tell yourself to calm down by getting out a book you like and
reading. Or pull up your journal file from "Classroom" online
and jot down ways to slow your mind to a manageable pace.

Ah, the audience. When you write essays, keep
your audience in mind. What emotions will people
feel while reading your essay? Remember, it is one
thing to write for friends; it is another to write for the
distinguished International Baccalaureate team of

scholastic judges.

However, you do have "assists." Just like an autopilot vehicle has intelligence sensors that can read the paint on the road, your own mind can forecast reactions of readers and detect emotions. For the best results, choose rhetorical appeals that engage and that fit your particular text and topic.

Think of how you feel when you read a short story or book that moves you. Maybe it changes your mind set, brings tears to your eyes, or opens you to a viewpoint that you previously would not have considered. Consider this example from Jules Verne's book *20,000 Leagues Under the Sea*: "On the 15th of March we were in the latitude of New Shetland and South Orkney. The captain told me that formerly numerous tribes of seals inhabited them, but English and American whalers, in their rage for destruction, massacred both old and young; thus, where there was once life and animation, they had left silence and death" (246). Pathos appeal, anybody?

Get your arms around Aristotle's appeals. These important Greek terms reflect four ways that an author uses *rhetorical strategies* to reach an audience and inspire involvement. The appeals ethos, pathos, logos, and kairos spur emotions and reactions.

So, this matters exactly why? Essentially, works of literature, online articles and columns, histories, and all other texts "succeed" only if they affect readers to some degree. Few writers put ideas on paper just to pass the time of day. They seek to communicate, persuade, inform, entertain, etc. An essay is the perfect vehicle for opinions and persuasion and enlightenment.

In writing nonfiction and fiction, you need to know how to use appeals effectively to achieve high-level writing proficiency. Whether you want to move readers to anger or frustration or heartbreak or fear, you absolutely don't want them to walk away from your essay unmoved.

For example, if you're writing an essay in which you intend to increase readers' awareness of the benefits of keeping a journal, show them why you know something about this (ethos) and what it will do to improve their lives (pathos). If a reader finishes your essay and responds with a grin and an "a-hah" moment, you hit the bull's-eye; however, if a reader sees no point in journaling, your essay failed to hit the mark. That's why we get do-overs. You can play around with word choices and sentence structure and descriptions until you zero in on the best way to convince readers that keeping a journal can make a dramatic difference. The words are in your mind; just pull them out and write the essay right.

"Rhetorical appeals won't be Greek to you anymore."

Touch people. Do your words get readers bent out of shape with discomfort? Misty-eyed? Eager to act? Great! A well-written essay draws readers in, and when it ends, they wish it hadn't. Just like a film or book that you can't savor long enough, a beautiful essay has a glow about it that will have readers staring at the words even after reading the last sentence. Just knowing that you can achieve that degree of investment can be a huge motivator to write.

Possessing thoughts that you want to share

is moving, and that feeling will not let you be a slacker. The Force in you will claw and scrape until some very cool words come bursting out, begging to be part of your essay.

Befriend them. Invite them into your "mind" community. It's all good fun, and that's the perch we want you to reach, the one where your writing comes so naturally that even you are astounded. *Is this really happening? Yes, indeed, it is.*

Then, you will get to experience a surge of adrenaline when you see your teacher or parent or classmate flinch, knowing that you were the one who wrote the terrific essay in their hands. The expression on their faces says, "Wow, I didn't know you had it in you." And your response is probably going to be, "Yeah, I didn't know I had it, either, but I'm glad I found out."

In fact, this is probably much like the emotion that 1800s impressionist artist Claude Monet felt the first time he saw admirers relishing his paintings. Maybe then and only then, he said, "Guess I do have an artist in me…" Even his own father was against Claude's pursuit of art, but talent eventually determined this painter's fate, and he became one of the world's most prolific and acclaimed artists ever. Guess dear old dad was wrong, right?

Appeals Won't Be Greek to You Anymore

Ethos: The appeal to ethics—ethos—is the act of convincing an audience that you are credible; otherwise, they won't listen to you. Trust is key. Many authors have credentials or backgrounds that allow them to establish instant ethos with readers. Sandra Cisneros, who wrote the novel *The House on Mango Street*, carries automatic credibility because she writes of being Mexican-American; thus, the reader knows the story comes from a place of experience. She writes, for example, "I am tired of looking at what we can't have" (Cisneros).

Another intriguing example is this one from *20,000 Leagues Under the Sea*, by Jules Verne, who writes, "Captain Nemo was terrible to hear; he was still more terrible to see. His face was deadly pale, with a spasm at his heart. For an instant it must have ceased to beat. His pupils were fearfully contracted. He did not *speak*, he *roared*, as, with his body thrown forward, he wrung the Canadian's shoulders. Then, leaving him, and turning to the ship of war, whose shot was still raining around him, he exclaimed with a powerful voice, 'Ah, ship of an accursed nation, you know who I am! I do not want your colors to know you by. Look and I will show you mine!'" (307).

In simple terms, *ethos* is the proof that an author knows whereof he speaks on a certain issue. Why do we believe that person? The author may rely on his good reputation or position as an authority. A classic example is an ad in which doctors endorse a product; this is an appeal to ethos that tells you, "Nine out of ten doctors recommend eating bear-claw pastries for breakfast." Anyway, with nothing else to go on, you're excited to hear the news, and you say, "Okay, those pastries must be good for me" and head for the nearest bakery. Of course, this crazy nutrition information reminds us that it is important to be a skeptical consumer of information; do not believe everything you read online. Verify!

In short, ethos encompasses credibility and ethics; pathos, emotions, and feelings; and logos, logic and reason. The philosopher Aristotle had the most faith in logos appeals simply because statistics, facts, and figures support that appeal. He believed that most people are rational; thus, the best way to reach them is with data, research, and evidence ("Ethos Defined").

Can You Feel It?

Pathos: "It's not so much that I like him as a person, God, but as a boy he's very handsome" (Blume 65). As you can see from this one-liner, author Judy Blume, in her phenomenal young adult novel *Are You There, God? It's Me, Margaret,* has an amazing ability to write in a way that touches young people. Simple words make an emphatic point.

"At the sight that met my eyes, my blood was changed into something exquisitely thin and icy" (47 Stevenson). In this line from *The Strange Case of Dr. Jekyll and Mr. Hyde*, you sense a mystery unfolding as the words "thin and icy" blood impart eeriness and a pathos blend of caution and paranoia.

Pathos: The pathos appeal spurs readers to empathize; it evokes feelings in audience members. Do you want to induce feelings of sadness, sorrow, happiness, or amusement? Writing tone and language go a long way toward promoting pathos in essays. You want readers to be "affected" by what you write so that their takeaway is an action or a new point of view or a lightening of spirit or a lifting of emotional state.

Empowered!

"It was all very well to say, "Drink me," but the wise little Alice was not going to do *that* in a hurry. For she had read several nice little stories about children who had got burnt and eaten up by wild beasts…all because they *would* not remember the simple rules their friends had taught them: that a red-hot poker will burn you if you hold it too long, and that if you cut your finger *very* deeply with a knife, it usually bleeds. And she had never forgotten that if you drink much from a bottle marked 'Poison,' it is almost certain to disagree with you, sooner or later" (13-14, *Alice in Wonderland*, by Lewis Carroll).

Fascinating!

Connect with a reader's empathy via pathos appeal, and you touch an emotional chord. For example, a TV ad that features thin, sick dogs invites viewers to adopt neglected canines and care for them until they are healthy again. The audience feels sorry for these dogs and either sends a check or seeks information on adoption. Logos and ethos appeal to a person's logic, but pathos appeals to feelings.

Appeal to Logic

Logos: The writer relies on logic to make a point and includes data or statistics to support the claim. Use reasoning, facts, and specifics to back up a logos appeal as you seek to convince readers. Of course, the information must be clear and relevant or no appeal works.

Here's a logos example: "Two-Bit reached into his back pocket for his prize possession. It was a jet-handled switchblade, ten inches long, that would flash open at a mere breath. It was the reward of two hours of walking aimlessly around a hardware store to divert suspicion. He kept it razor sharp" (Hinton, S.E. *The Outsiders* 125. Excerpts from THE OUTSIDERS by S.E. Hinton, copyright © 1967, renewed 1995 by S.E. Hinton. Used by permission of Viking Children's Books, an imprint of Penguin Young Readers Group, a division of Penguin Random House LLC. All rights reserved).

This switchblade description makes sense to readers and helps advance the story.

Is It Kairos Time?

Kairos: A word that is Greek for "right time," kairos refers to an argument's timeliness. Often, timing is everything in order for an argument to succeed. Would you place a fragrance ad in *Computer*

World Magazine? (Actually, that might be a good idea.)

At any rate, kairos refers to a persuasive message being delivered at the right time. An example would be an ad during the Olympics that talks about patriotism; the time and place are ideal.

Combo Appeals

In an entertaining Old Navy commercial, TV star Julia Louis-Dreyfus plays a snobby mom whose well-dressed son just wishes he could wear cool clothes like other kids in the commercial. This ad has ethos, pathos, and logos working together; it's funny, effective, and has a celebrity to make it authoritative and even the extra plus of a television icon people love. Everyone finds Julia Louis-Dreyfus likable to the nth degree, and no one can get enough of her wit and sass; check out this great first-day-of-school ad on YouTube.

Rhetorical appeals are also persuasive techniques. As a writer, you use them as modes of persuasion to convince readers that your argument is sound. Kairos comes into play least often in writing essays because it refers to a message sent at an opportune time, fulfilling the adage "strike while the iron is hot."

How Appeals Work

Ethos, pathos, logos, and kairos help you establish strong links to your readers and evoke certain emotions. To become proficient at essay writing, it's important to learn how to use appeals effectively. Of course, some writers instinctively draw on these appeals. Think William Shakespeare for one and Pat Conroy (*The Prince of Tides*) for another.

To "get" what this influencing mechanism really means, read authors who are experts at rhetorical appeals. One is Truman Capote, best known for *In Cold Blood*, a novel in which this author skillfully "makes" the reader care about two killers and how they evolve into despicable men. He does the impossible of framing prose that spotlights empathetically the misfortunes of the killers almost as successfully as those of the victims.

This book defines the word "page-turner." No one can put it down—even if something itchy in them really wants to toss it and pretend such people never existed. Of course, the fact that *ICB* is based-on-a-true-story helps. Readers know that these monsters did kill, and there is something earthshaking about studying their histories to discover the "why" behind their sins. Example: When the character Perry recalls his own father's account of Perry as a boy, he walks away thinking that the biography "always set racing a stable of emotions—self-pity in the lead, love and hate running evenly at first, the latter ultimately pulling ahead. And most of the memories it released were unwanted…" (*In Cold Blood*, by Truman Capote, copyright © 1965 by Penguin; excerpt used by permission of Penguin Random House LLC. All rights reserved).

Chapter Fourteen:
Write Rhetorical Essays

Tip for the Day: When you write essays, shake off that cozy yet codependent relationship with your phone. You actually don't need a laptop or phone at arm's length because you have the perfect creativity machine between your ears. Use that wonderful mind. Not only is it 100% exclusively yours, but it's 100% better than anything you could ever imagine finding (and copying) off social media. Smartphones feel like vital organs, of course, but that doesn't have to detract from your inherent genius.

Feel. Think. Sigh. Cry. Simmer. Scream. If a

book hits its mark, it will evoke emotions in you that make you glad you read it—or mad that it irritated you. A writer sets out to persuade or inspire or entertain or inform or antagonize or make you angry, sad, happy, or content.

No one goes through the many hours of writing a book to end up with readers closing the book halfway through. A writer writes so that readers will act or react, experience, or emote. You are disappointed when you fail to finish a marathon; joyful when you win a gold medal in the Olympics for water polo; unhappy about dropping out of gymnastics training after ten years of it; and updated

intellectually when you read about voter I.D. for U.S. elections. All of these revelations come after a writer's rhetoric touches you; the words make a difference.

To write a rhetorical analysis essay, you need to understand that "rhetoric" is "the art of effective or persuasive speaking or writing, especially the use of figures of speech (or figurative language)." A rhetorical essay requires the purposeful and intentional use of rhetoric to influence readers. Every word has a purpose. Every word counts.

Let's say you're writing an essay on racism in the novel *Adventures of Huckleberry Finn*, by Mark Twain (1884). Your winning trifecta will show how the author conveys an anti-prejudice (or anti-bias) message through

- Figurative language
- An anecdote (a short story) from the book
- Rhetorical appeals that touch readers, who then empathize with the message.

Sample topic sentence: Although Huck Finn accepts his community's attitude of prejudice toward blacks and grows up believing they are right, author Mark Twain, in his novel *Adventures of Huckleberry Finn,* uses figurative language and pathos to spotlight a contrarian view, the importance of tolerance.

In writing a rhetorical analysis essay, you explain to the readers of your essay exactly how rhetorical appeals allow readers to appreciate an author's credibility (ethos), experience emotions that the book evokes (pathos), accept facts and statistics that prove the point logically (logos), and, in some cases, see that the text's timing makes it relevant (kairos).

Keep these in mind when you write an essay:

- Ethos: What credentials does the writer have to write this article or story?
- Pathos: What does the writing make the reader feel? Anger, sorrow, pity?
- Logos: How logical is the argument?
- Kairos: Is the timing spot-on?

In a rhetorical analysis, explore the target audience, tone, voice, imagery, sentence structure, and diction—and tell your readers how the author uses rhetorical strategies to influence readers. In rhetorical analysis essays written by high school students (see the following), note how the writers examine aspects of the author's writing and explain how appeals evoke certain desired responses in readers. Also, these students discuss how tone, diction, sentence structure, mood, and imagery set apart the particular texts (short story, novel, etc.) as exceptional. Putting these elements into play, a writer can turn out a rhetorical analysis that resonates.

Here is one senior's introduction to a rhetorical essay. As you read, notice how word choice, sentence structure, and voice make this introduction memorable.

WWII Evil: *Unbroken* and *The Shining*

Think serial killers. Or the Holocaust. Or any old homicidal maniac. Truly, evil is a wickedly tough concept to fathom, yet provocative, which explains the success of the biography *Unbroken,* by Laura Hillenbrand, and the gothic horror film *The Shining,* directed by Stanley Kubrick and derived from Stephen King's novel. Both works examine the theme "man's inhumanity to man." *Unbroken* spotlights atrocities that prisoner-of-war Louis Zamperini endures. While their protagonists struggle against abject horrors, Kubrick and Hillenbrand catalog mankind's cruelties in a brilliant film and an excellent book. Two formats serve up tears and treachery—one visual, one text, both heart-wrenching. This film and biography, backlit by the Holocaust, are reminders that evils are, as Kubrick says, "the world's grotesque products" (Cocks, "Cinema and Me"). Thankfully, though, literature and films elevate problems and inspire humankind to think, plan, and act.

187

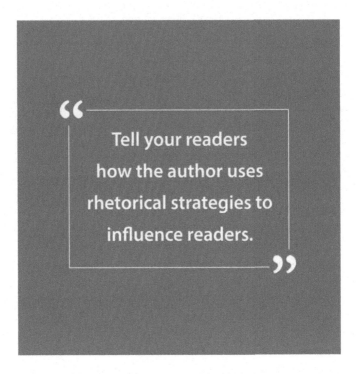

"Tell your readers how the author uses rhetorical strategies to influence readers."

Breaking Down Woolf's "Two Meals"

Before having her students dive into writing a rhetorical analysis essay, California teacher Gwen Gaylord asks her AP English students to sort the text pieces: speaker, subject, occasion, audience, overarching argument, and global issue. What follows here is an excerpt from a senior's take on the elements of "Two Meals," as he figures out a way to approach writing a rhetorical essay.

Speaker. The speaker is English author Virginia Woolf, who has a way of mocking society's roles that is almost as successful as satirist Jonathon Swift's ability to mock society's woes in "A Modest Proposal." Her chief trait illustrated in "Two Meals" is an ability to dissect a wrong and lay it bare for all to see. Ethos, a rhetorical appeal based on the credibility of the author, resonates in "Two Meals" because readers of that era (1929) know that this author is intelligent as well as a feminist force.

Subject. In "Two Meals," Woolf contrasts a three-course lunch for Oxbridge men with a dinner at Fernham women's college. The former is a sumptuous feast "fit for a king," while the latter is a meal that one might consume at a beggar's table. By showing the discrepancies in the foods offered, she spotlights the stark differences in the way men and women are regarded in that time period.

Occasion. The exigence for what Woolf is talking about at this moment is that she is a guest at two meals—a lunch served elegantly at a men's college and a dinner slapped onto the table of a women's college. In the greater context of her work, this is just one more example of her worldview, in which she observes that men have a loftier role in society than women. All men are created equal, but women—not so much.

Audience. The type of individual who would be most receptive to the speaker's words is any woman who has empathy for the women's movement. Woolf is a feminist, and she uses this occasion to point out what is wrong with serving two very different kinds of meals to two genders that both deserve respect. A traditional woman would be less inclined to find this comparison outrageous.

Overarching argument. The central claim Woolf makes in "Two Meals" is that it is ludicrous to serve a spectacular feast at a men's college and a meager meal for the residents of a women's school. To insinuate that men are more important in society than men is a thorny statement that Woolf does not accept as the final word. Logos comes into play because the reader must think about whether it makes sense—the discrepancy in a meal like this and a lesser one that might be served for those considered lesser human beings. Writer Sarah Schaffer, in "Dining Well on Woolf," says that powerful people usually do not "deign to discuss the particulars of a succulent piece of quail or the lightness of a perfectly cooked souffle, preferring instead to jabber about the stock market or their pet poodles" (Schaffer). But Woolf, who is capitulating to the novelty of food as a topic, writes eloquently about the disparities in foods that college cooks serve to women and men.

Global issue. The large-scale social topic explored in "Two Meals" is that men get preferred status in society over women. This is evident worldwide at the time of this writing, and it is still evident today in many countries although U.S. women have made strides. Knowing that women were not taken seriously in literary circles, Woolf still sets high standards for herself because "A Room of One's Own" was published in October 1929, a time when "feminist writing was so little in vogue as to be effectively moribund, when the feminist movement, connected as it had come to be almost exclusively with female suffrage, considered its work finished" (Gordon). Also, people were distracted by economic problems. Wall Street investors were leaping from windows in despair, and Mussolini was a force for evil.

Clearly, the dramatic differences in the two meals are notable. The one delivered to the men is elegant and complex; the one delivered to the women is plain and bland. In the first description, Woolf uses metaphors and similes to rhapsodize on the excellence of the taste and the splendid presentation of the meal. The description of the women's dinner sounds as woeful as the food served. The writing intrigues readers as Woolf uses figurative language to make taste buds savor foods possibly never before eaten. Even the reactions at the end of the meals reflect the levels of satisfaction in those who consume the food. While we read that the men "sunk among the cushions in the window-seat" and settle in to enjoy the atmosphere, the women exit the dining area quickly.

The minimal meal is symbolic of women's roles in society; they were homemakers and mothers, and society treated them as if they were second-class. Woolf represents it as a given that the college men "deserve" classy food, and the women should not expect more than bland food because spoiling is what males deserve, not females. She is being ironic, however.

Pathos appeal is apparent throughout. The reader begins to feel angry that women are treated as if they were of minor value. Men symbolize privilege; women represent practicality. The writing style is a flowery and lengthy narrative for the men's meal. The writing style for the women's meal is clipped and staccato. Similarly, the tone is luxurious for the first and plodding for the second. The challenge in Woolf's mood is an underlying feel of resentment, in which she looks at how the genders are treated and argues its wrongness. Women, in essence, are background music for men's important lives of producing, leading, and discussing. With well-chosen words, Woolf examines men's and women's positions in society and questions the pecking order. Her tone has a rebellious sound even as she understates her fury. She reports the differences. She loathes the truth of it.

As Woolf attacks the two meals in "Two Meals," she writes an unforgettable treatise on food-as-bias, and many writers are convinced that "Virginia Woolf, one of the greatest modernist novelists and feminist writers, will go down in history not for her perfectly shaped sentences but for her understanding of the subtleties of sauce and gravy" (Schaffer). Ironically, though, in the same way a psychiatrist in a movie will remind someone that their issue "is not about the soup," Woolf definitely is not quibbling about the value of quail over soup; rather, she bemoans a societal structure that minimizes women. She knew how it felt to be treated as if she were inconsequential because she lived in the early days of feminism.

Try Your Hand at Rhetorical Analysis

In your English class, you will read some articles, short stories, and books analytically; in other words, you're not just breezing through the chapters. Instead, you are looking for specific aspects of the text, and later you'll be writing about these as elements of what makes the particular book or poem or short story successful. Authors use setting, tone, and figurative language to make characters come alive and to entice readers to get caught up in the tale until they can shut out the noisy world and just enjoy reading.

What you are not doing when you do rhetorical analysis is writing a book report, like you did in the fifth grade. You are examining why the work of literature works so well and detecting what elements of the author's toolbox enabled him to engage readers successfully. You may be asking, "And how can I do that if I don't like the book?" The answer is this: If you're assigned a particular text, that's what your teacher wants you to read and analyze; thus, don't spend much time dwelling on the fact that it's not your favorite story. The process of analysis is the point, and you can pull that off even when the book or short story or play isn't one that you find compelling.

Essentially, every story always boils down to what happens, where it happens, why it happens, when it happens, and to whom it happens. A story's nuts and bolts include:

Plot: the events of the story or what actually happens.

Characters: the people who populate the story and act and think and entertain you, the reader. The protagonist (main character) is the one you root for;

the antagonist is the one you "boo."

Conflict: Without conflict, conflict, conflict, there is no story. The protagonist seeks to accomplish something and keeping this from happening are actions of the antagonists, presenting one obstacle after another.

Setting: The period (era), the location, weather, and the political and social and economic atmosphere of the time.

Narrator: This is the storyteller.

Theme: The story's message or main idea; what the author wants to communicate that is a universal truth or concern about life and society.

Point of view: how the narrative unfolds. This does not mean your perspective on life, better known as your "voice."

Five types of narrative point of view are: first person, second person, third-person omniscient, third-person limited, and third-person objective.

First person: Use this one when the story is all about you. You want to use the pronouns "my," "I," and "me," and you're writing about something that happened to you. A book that always comes to mind when speaking of first person POV is Harper Lee's *To Kill a Mockingbird*, which the child Scout Finch narrates, or J.D. Salinger's *Catcher in the Rye*, narrated by Holden Caulfield.

If you are writing a narrative essay, you might word it this way: *When I was seven years old, I looked around at my chaotic family and decided someone needed to be in charge.* What's special about this POV is that it's so easy to relate to the character this way. This is the coziest point of view, no doubt about it. However, the writer is limited because being in just one character's head makes it harder to tell a story. In first person, the narrator describes absolutely everything from his/her point of view.

Second person: The reader is front and center with second-person POV. Pronouns that you use are "you" and "yours." The reader becomes part of the story. "You never thought the day would come when you would turn down a trip to the beach on a hot summer day, but the threats on the way to Crystal Cove were frightening. You were too afraid to take the chance of stopping to enjoy some leisure time."

Third-person POV: A narrative is often written in third person, and that requires: "he," "she," "it," "they," "them," "their," "his," "hers," and "theirs." Within the third-person category are three options. Most often used is third-person omniscient. Think of the word's definition, which is "all-knowing," and that way you'll never forget what it means.

There are three different third-person points of view. We are going to start with the most common one, third-person omniscient. The narrator is positioned above it all and knows the thoughts of all characters in the story. This may mean using multiple characters' perspectives, so one chapter is entitled "Mabel," and the next one "John," and another one "Jean-Paul." The novel *Pride and Prejudice*, by Jane Austen, is an example of third-person omniscient.

Many authors turn to third-person omniscient because it's so flexible. It doesn't have the limitations of other POVs.

Third-person limited: This one has one character offering thoughts and ideas. It is handy because you aren't merely in the one head (yours) of first person. Third-person limited lets an author relate feelings as well as make observations of the book's little cosmos.

J.K. Rowling gets readers wound up in her storytelling by using third-person limited POV. Typically, she makes events resonate by using Harry Potter's sights, sounds, feelings, and experiences.

Third-person limited example: On December 1, 1955, in Montgomery, Alabama, African American activist Rosa Parks refused to give up her seat on a bus to a white man as she took a memorable stand in the civil rights movement.

Writers favor third-person omniscient and third-person limited because both make it easy to help the reader develop empathy for characters. The goal is to ensure that you, the reader, cannot read the novel without becoming engaged.

Third-person objective POV: here, the author has the narrative take on the perspective of an objective outsider; point of view tells the story from the perspective of a total outsider.

Example: The look on Ariana Grande's face reveals how carefully she is sizing up the other judges on the TV show "The Voice" in order to figure out how she fits in. Mystery and distance are pretty much guaranteed if you choose to use third-person objective. You are standing by, telling a tale.

Some writers change points of view within a story. There are readers who like this style; others find it disconcerting.

Follow the Steps of Analysis

Write a one-paragraph introduction that sets out what you want to prove in your essay. You include the TAG (title, author, genre) and set up the issue you will explain. Make it clear why this is a topic of value and show what is notable about your reasoning. Hint that you will present a surprising angle or truth. After reading this introduction, readers should know what you'll be discussing and the path you plan to take. Typically, in a five-paragraph essay, the last sentence of the intro is the thesis sentence (your "promise" of what you will do in this essay). Do not make wild assertions or nonsensical claims. Stay on point.

Turn the arguments outlined in the intro into three paragraphs. Begin each with a clear, strong topic sentence. In the topic sentence, you say what the paragraph will cover and how you will accomplish that. Deal with one point only and don't add off-topic information. Then go on to the next paragraph and repeat this process. Check to make sure you've included GLUE (transition words and phrases that link one paragraph to the next).

Write a conclusion that sums up what you've presented, as if to say the whole point one more time for good measure. Rather than summarizing the paragraphs, synthesize them by telling how, together, these lead to the obvious conclusion. Don't pad with new ideas. Try to make your final paragraph dynamic but not fantastical. Choose words carefully. Glance back to see if you've done a good job of repeating what you said in the thesis sentence without repeating the same words. Paraphrase, in other words.

Write a *Frankenstein* Rhetorical Analysis

Write a multi-paragraph rhetorical analysis essay that explains how the author Mary Shelley uses theme, tone, and characterization to argue that too much ambition can prove devastating.

In the novel *Frankenstein*, author Mary Shelley spotlights the complex human condition as she captures a dramatic standoff that evolves when protagonist Victor Frankenstein goes on a quest to test his own ability to create a monster. As he relies on ambition and selfishness to reach his goals, he grows increasingly alienated from other human beings until it becomes clear that the book's characterization and tone will display cunningly the theme of alienation grounded in things both sinister and supernatural. Amid a showcase of monstrosities, Mary Shelley includes the horrid knowledge Frankenstein plumbs in an effort to follow his ambition, create the monster, and ignore all who get in his way. Though Victor at first seems relatively "normal" to the reader, his ill-fated quest leads to a surprising end game in which he loathes his own creation. Thus, the author offers a triumphant treatment of theme, characterization, and tone as the trifecta of elements moving this 1818 novel from the realm of bizarre fantasy to prized classic.

Ironically, Victor Frankenstein starts out innocently enough when he admits his heart glows "with an enthusiasm which elevates me to heaven, for nothing contributes so much to tranquillize the mind as a steady purpose—a point on which the soul may fix its intellectual eye" (2). However, when he is hit by schizophrenic blowback from meeting his challenge, Frankenstein must face the truth—that he has created "a monster," with unintended consequences, including an oddly "human" ability to haunt Frankenstein and his monster. Remarkably, alienation as a theme, proves to be of consequence. Even though critics largely view this novel as a patchwork quilt of voices and tenses, the mashup texture also makes it a vehicle for brandishing social alienation as both a cause of evil and a punishment for evil.

With the monster anchoring this story, a darkly mysterious tone accompanies Victor Frankenstein's eerie experiment. From a mix of chemicals and stolen body parts, the yield is a grotesque monster that morphs into a stunning replica of monstrosity. In fact, the monster itself has a shadowy proclivity all his own that becomes apparent when he emphasizes his own self-loathing as feelings of revenge begin to consume him. Feeling alienated from society because he looks monstrous, the monster first recognizes that he is ugly not through someone else's judgment but through his own: "when I viewed myself in a transparent pool…I was filled with the bitterest sensations." Specifically, this novel sends a message that a person becomes alienated from others chiefly by gradual alienation from himself. Complicating matters further, the tone goes bitter when both Victor

Frankenstein and the monster view their alienation from God as a crime and a punishment.

Dangerous ambition corrupts, and this theme is well portrayed in Mary Shelley's *Frankenstein* via extreme characterization. Had Frankenstein not set out to create a monster, he would not have ended up on the slippery slope of conflicted feelings about his own character. Thus, the author notes that Frankenstein believes he erred so drastically in choosing to create a monster, that his "sin" can be likened to worlds colliding, proof positive of an ambitious streak that is more injury than inspiration. Imagining that he is a Satan-like archangel who aspires to be an omniscient ruler, Victor loses touch with reality as his ego grows so overblown that he dramatizes his worth and attests to being the devil. At the same time, he is haunted by the results of his experiment and his shortsightedness in failing to think of "next steps." Thus, he urges others to learn from him, "if not by my precepts, at least by my example, how dangerous is the acquirement of knowledge and how much happier that man is who believes his native town to be the world, than he who aspires to become greater than his nature will allow" (38). In these words, Victor likens the acquisition of dicey knowledge to ill-gotten gains that are doomed to rock his world and taint his achievement. To flesh out the

theme, Mary Shelley delves onto the dark side.
Frankenstein says, "When I run over the frightful
catalogue of my sins, I cannot believe that I am the
same creature whose thoughts were once filled with
sublime and transcendent visions of the beauty and
the majesty of goodness. But it is even so; the fallen
angel becomes a malignant devil" (4). With these
words, he emphasizes how affected he is by having
created a monster, but he cannot shake the inability to
find ways "to solve" his problem. Essentially, his
disappointment suggests that most things a person
strives for fail to be as fulfilling as expected, leaving
the seeker devastated. Frankenstein notes, "For this I
had deprived myself of rest and health. I had desired
it with an ardour (sic) that far exceeded moderation;
but now that I had finished, the beauty of the dream
vanished, and breathless horror and disgust filled my
heart" (42).

Finally, the tone, theme, and characterization, are
three factors ruling the day in a lesson that extreme
ambition devastates. Frankenstein ends up dead,
leaving the monster to fend for himself in the world.
Therefore, he sums it up by describing his own
loathing for himself: "You hate me; but your
abhorrence cannot equal that with which I regard
myself." Thus, in effect, the end game to alienation is
a kamikaze moment of self-destruction. Chasing the

monster, Frankenstein ensures his own demise, and meanwhile, the monster opts for suicide. He makes them both miserable, as is clarified by Frankenstein's own reaction to his creation: "…[a] flash of lightning illuminated the object and discovered its shape plainly to me; its gigantic stature, and the deformity of its aspect, more hideous than belongs to humanity, instantly informed me that it was the wretch, the filthy demon to whom [he] had given life" (60).

In the end, Frankenstein's tragic flaw is that he is able to prioritize ambition over duties he owes to those around him. He is not good as a friend or a creator; so, is he is a failure? One who disappoints himself, then, perhaps is destined to disappoint others in his life. "The labours (sic) of men of genius, however erroneously directed, scarcely ever fail in ultimately turning to the solid advantage of mankind" (34). He adds with a wry disgust, "Learn from me, if not by my precepts, at least by my example, how dangerous is the acquirement of knowledge and how much happier that man is who believes his native town to be the world, than he who aspires to become greater than his nature will allow" (38). His creation, then, ruins his life. As Victor articulates, "When I looked around, I saw and heard of none like me. Was I, the monster, a blot upon the earth from which all men fled and whom all men disowned?" (105). By the end of the tale, readers undoubtedly note the foreshadowing that suggests that this monster will turn on its maker. The hellish existence that emerges for both of them is significant in that "from that moment [he] declared everlasting war against the species, and more than all, against [Frankenstein] who had formed [him] and sent [him] forth to this insupportable misery" (121). Thus, theme, characterization, and tone, aptly move this 1818 novel from being just another book to a classic that profoundly moves readers.

Next Prompt, Please

We asked a high school sophomore to write a rhetorical essay on changing women's roles and to make sure to use ethos appeal. Notice how this rhetorical device changes the essay's tone from informative to moving.

Rhetorical Strategies Reflect Feminism's Trends

Touch up your makeup. Put a ribbon in your hair. Clear away clutter. Have dinner ready. Prepare the children. Minimize noise. Do not greet your husband with complaints. Believe it or not, these are actual "tips" for wives from a 1953 magazine article, "How to Be a Good Wife" (Dr. Nancy website). Shocking, all right, and anyone who shows that list to a 2021 woman hears laughter, guaranteed. Rules such as "have a cool or warm drink ready for him" and "keep the children quiet" show that Americans then had radically different expectations for stay-at-home moms/wives from the ones that exist today.

Apparently, changes wrought by '60s feminists were long overdue. However, like most issues, one might say "not so fast" about drawing positive conclusions. Why? Simply put, women did join the working world in droves, true, but many who did so over the decades later decided that the upshot was adding *more* work (fulltime jobs) to their existing responsibilities. The perceived goal of "equality" with men did not pan out, in other words, because the household and parenting duties remained where they had always been, right there in women's laps.

Clearly, today, the women's movement is not a done deal. In her book *The Rise of Neoliberal Feminism* (Oxford University Press, 2018, Material reproduced through permission of the Licensor through PLSclear©), author Catherine Rottenberg argues that Americans are witnessing a brand of "neoliberal feminism" spawned by the feminist texts *Lean In*, by Sheryl Sandberg, and "Why Women Still Can't Have It All," by Anne-Marie Slaughter (*Atlantic* magazine). Rottenberg contends that today's new feminist accepts full responsibility for herself and seeks a pleasing work/family balance that is "based on a cost-benefit calculus" (Rottenberg, Material reproduced through permission of the Licensor through PLSclear©). Having analyzed mommy blogs and television offerings, she sees a new breed of "aspirational women" dedicated to a happy work-family balance but also intent on cultivating a pleasant equilibrium between child-rearing duties and professional goals. This means many women have abandoned the goals of equal rights and liberation, which historically informed feminism because neoliberalism reduces everything to market calculations. However, women of color, the poor, and immigrant women, are the care-workers who make it possible for professional women to achieve balance. Thus, neoliberal feminism legitimizes exploitation of women, and that leaves Rottenberg asking for a renewal of feminism as a social justice movement (Rottenberg, Material reproduced with permission of the Licensor through PLSclear©).

From a contrarian viewpoint, though, there is blowback from the outcry of women who are not fans of Gloria Steinem-based feminism launched in the '60s. Writer Anne-Marie Slaughter points out that women truthfully cannot "have it all" because "a big impediment to achieving a work-life balance is the 'time macho' culture of the professional world.

Women face the pressure to put in 'face time' at the office—arriving early, staying late, and working weekends, but this does not necessarily work well for a woman rearing children" (Susan Jones). In fact, according to the U.S. Bureau of Labor Statistics, "about 55 percent of American mothers employed full time do some housework on an average day, while only 18 percent of employed fathers do. Even if you control for the fact that moms with full-time jobs tend to work fewer hours than dads with full-time jobs, working women with children are still doing a week and a half more of 'second shift'[3] work each year than male partners" (Grose). Men and women of 2021 can find humor in the "Good Wife" article, which a '50s-era home economics textbook featured, but they must also acknowledge that gender roles remain today are still lopsided in men's favor. Even as big players in the work force, most women continue to do the heavy lifting at home, while men's records on "pitching in" are spotty at best.

In fact, millions of moms/wives who skeptically examine "gains" of the feminist movement cannot

---

[3] "Second Shift" was popularized by sociologist Arlie Hochschild in her book *The Second Shift*. The term refers to childcare and household duties that professional women do after work (the First Shift).

help feeling compelled to put those in perspective with the realities of how family lifestyles really worked out. *Britannica* cites feminist Betty Friedan's 1962 book *The Feminine Mystique* as one of the first to declare that not all women enjoyed being confined to cooking meals and rearing children, and this inspired women to get jobs and seek equal footing with men. Obviously, knitting sox, making soup, and helping kids with homework were not the only things women could do well, and U.S. women spoke loudly, shunning stereotypical roles. And while few people alive today would applaud the "Good Wife" standards, it is undeniable that the dynamic that feminism put in place has not worked out as expected. Nitty-gritty household jobs did not go away, and most working moms cannot afford a cook, a housekeeper, or a chauffeur for children. Thus, today's landscape features a host of women who *do not* agree that the women's movement improved matters for females. A second salary did make more families affluent or at least middle class, but many men still expected women to continue housekeeping, cooking, bill-paying, childcare, recreation directing, and budgeting. The upshot is that many American women who have no "help" in the home still juggle traditional responsibilities along with fulltime jobs. They wonder: exactly how are they better off than

'50s women?

Apparently, they are not, and that leaves many American women disgruntled. "My parenting and professional responsibilities make this 'Good Wife' list even funnier," says Mia Mahoney, who is an accountant and mom of kids ages three, five, and seven. "Marriages today are partnerships, and that means 'How to Be a Good Wife' would appear in print today only if accompanied by 'How to Be a Good Husband.'" Certainly, Mia Mahoney is not praising the rewards of the feminism.

Finally, the real question posed by Jessica Grose, author of the article "Cleaning: The Final Feminist Frontier," is: Were families really better off back when women executed wifely duties for their husband-kings? Or is today's version of "equality" ultimately better for both women and men?

The fact is, most U.S. women and men do not share household chores equally, and the saying "man may work from sun to sun, but a woman's work is never done" still resonates. However, women are not afraid to complain about unfairness. Men, perplexed by it all but still unskilled at household chores, freely endorse the saying "*Happy wife, happy life.*" And some may even offer to bathe the kids.

In the end, for the women's movement to survive, people have to face real-life scenarios, not glowing hypotheticals. Women rearing kids, doing household work, and holding down fulltime jobs are not happy campers simply because multitasking 24/7 is exhausting. However, to improve matters, Americans can spotlight favorably those men who do partner successfully and applaud their achievements. Truly, even badly dressed toddlers and imperfect mopping cannot mar a shared, universal desire to make roles more consistent in U.S. society. Strong and optimistic, many American pairs, after revising home/parenting responsibilities in the cold light of what really happens, stand ready to make equality a reality and not just a word on a protest poster.

Note Points of Analysis:

The many sources cited appeal to ethos and build the argument. Citing sources builds credibility by giving expert opinions as well as facts and statistics to support the claim. These include: *Lean In*, "Why Women Still Can't Have It All," *Feminine Mystique*, "How to Be a Good Wife," "Cleaning: The Final Feminist Frontier," and *The Second Shift*. Adding to the ethos, the writer illustrates the success of Jessica Grose's "Cleaning: The Final Feminist Frontier," in her strong appeals to logos, offering a logical progression of ideas from experts as well as factual material. Furthermore, by spotlighting men's lack of chore-sharing as problematic, this student writer invokes pathos. Emotionally charged words stir sympathy, including "disgruntled" and "cold light of what really happens." At the same time, she does not prove so relentless in word choices that she loses her male audience; for example, she refers to "imperfect mopping" rather than just saying that men are bad at doing household chores. Even a simple euphemism such as this changes the tone of the essay and leaves the reader feeling hopeful.

Finally, the writer asks, in essence, if proper sponge-squeezing really matters. In addition, she suggests that the women's movement stays relevant only if feminists deal successfully with the truth of how their movement has played out in suburbia. She implies that otherwise, this movement falls off the radar screen because no one can expect women to wear twenty hats and call it stylish.

Above, we illustrate how rhetorical appeals come into play and readers are moved. A high school senior wrote this rhetorical essay.

Moving Right Along

Epic essays that invoke rhetorical appeals make audiences feel true emotions. Whether it's anger or frustration or heartbreak or fear you seek to inspire, you're going to use words that move and affect readers. Furthermore, studying great works of fiction and nonfiction can help you choose rhetorical appeals masterfully. For example, would you argue that intellectually disabled Lennie in *Of Mice and Men* was doomed from birth to a miserable fate? Readers would wince at the thought that limited mental capacity seals a person's fate, and that is exactly the point that you want them to consider. What happens to the Lennies of this world?

As you write, your goal is to make the audience feel something, do something, or consider something. Offer examples and reasons. A well-written essay draws readers in. When it ends, they wish it hadn't. Just like you savor an outstanding film or book, a beautiful essay has a magnificence that makes readers keep staring at the words long after the last sentence has been read. This is one thing that motivates writers to achieve exactly that.

See if you can identify the types of appeals in these sentences:

"Gale Virtual Reference Library delivers a wealth of eBook reference content in a database" (Newport Beach Public Library Online Databases). *Appeal: Ethos—most people view a librarian as a trustworthy person.*

What appeals were used by author F. Scott Fitzgerald in the following excerpt? "For a moment the last sunshine fell with romantic affection upon her glowing face…then the glow faded, each light deserting her with lingering regret, like children leaving a pleasant street at dusk" (Fitzgerald 14, excerpt from *The Great Gatsby*©, by F. Scott Fitzgerald, reproduced with permission of The Licensor through PLSclear©). *Would you characterize the above appeal as pathos, and if so, does it evoke a melancholy feeling or is it closer to sorrow?*

"She had drunk a quantity of champagne, and during the course of the song she had decided, ineptly, that everything was very, very sad—she was not only singing, she was weeping, too. Whenever there was a pause in the song, she filled it with gasping, broken sobs, and then took up the lyric again in a quavering soprano. The tears coursed down her cheeks—not freely, however, for when they came into contact with her heavily beaded eyelashes they assumed an inky color, and pursued the rest of the way in slow black rivulets" (Fitzgerald 51, excerpt from *The Great Gatsby*©, by F. Scott Fitzgerald, reproduced with permission of The Licensor through PLSclear©).

Is this pathos? Are you amused or is your emotion pity?

Chapter Fifteen:
Sample "Casual English"

Tip for the Day: Now that we have filled your head with a zillion essay ideas, ask yourself if you would accept a "mission impossible." Are you ready for a hard-core, super-tough challenge? If so, read on. This chapter is for those of you who are comfortable writing in the classroom, on a boat, behind a moat. For anyone who loves to write, the "casual essay" is a don't-miss, but writing one requires an all-new creativity retreat.

As you have learned more about essay writing, one little niggling thought may have been dancing around in the back of your mind. Why do I have to bother with avoiding contractions and "I" and "you" if I'm a really good writer who can make it work even in a school essay? That's a valid question, but the fact is, author control of writing style is critical, and the success of writing without borders ends up wholly dependent on a writer's voice.

Over centuries, many writers have meshed formal writing with informal, so it's not like this is a brand-new notion. The key is in not confusing this "looser" form of English for a cross between the speedy texts you tap out for a friend and a well-written column by a published author. Those two would not blend well, ever.

Really, "casual English" has specific, critical components, including excellent word choice that imparts a uniquely quirky beauty, elegant sentence structure, great ideas, and textured style. Really, it's like having a one-of-a-kind banana split that you never even knew existed. Taste its supremely delicious nuances, and somehow you know, that raucous flavor has ruined you for any ordinary banana split for the rest of your life. But it was worth it.

On the other hand, tradition will continue to demand that students deliver the *formal* essay in its *formal* package. However, there may be boldness in you that says, "what the heck" and tries to write in a way that is genuinely reflective of you as an individual.

In fact, one quasi-compromise between the two extremes—formal and informal essay writing, is to come up with your own hybrid approach. How about one that has the required elements in place but also ventures into forbidden territory by using a colloquialism that would make any reader smile—or a sentence "departure" that makes even a high court of essay appeals person pause and consider its merit?

In the infamous Extended Essay, required for International Baccalaureate diploma-seeking students, any divergence from the "norm" makes you run the risk of having an essay dinged for "lack of appropriate formality" or even "lightweight and jargon-filled." It's easy to imagine the many textures and hues of possible criticisms. Hence, the point is this: If you love to write, you can't let the powers-that-be slow you to a snail's crawl if you are inclined to take on this tantalizing "casual essay" and do it well. Remember, though, that unless you deliver a spectacular piece of writing, it is easier for a critic to mark you down than to praise your audacity.

So, maybe the answer is not being afraid to throw in a "you" here and a "can't" there, simply because it sounds natural in what you're writing. Then, if you don't overdo your style risks, teachers and writing judges will perceive your deviations as deliberate and not accidental. Trying to maneuver your way into the madly successful, chat-esque language of a columnist like Joan Didion or David Brooks is no slam-dunk, but you won't get the death penalty for sticking your neck out on paper. As my mother used to say, "when you're worried or fearful, think of the worst thing that can happen, and if you can live with that, you're going to be fine."

No one ever went to the Emergency Room for delving into casual writing. Besides, the average writer out there has already suffered rejections galore and has become a sturdy person who can live through an earthquake only to respond blithely, "it happens."

The joy of word-shopping, is that this really does amount to a brainstorm free-for-all. No one understands what you're doing as a writer, anyway. Thus, who will fault you for off-roading? Our message, then, is: Take a journey. Go on a quest. Don't let Harrison Ford be the only one who gets to trudge through raging rapids to grab the Holy Grail. Who knows? "Casual English" may end up being the route that takes you where you want to go as a writer. Discover yourself, your voice, your pathway. Take Robert Frost's "Road Not Taken," and let it make all the difference in your writing (Frost).

Author note: The essay excerpt in Chapter Twelve is an example of Casual English because it combines formal and informal writing; the essay won a "6" of 7 on the highly competitive IB writing exam.

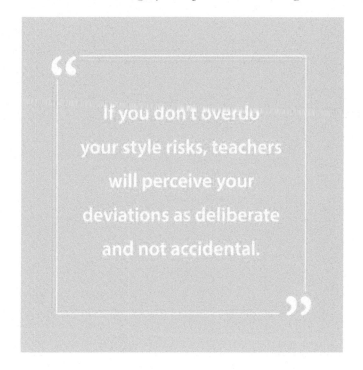

" If you don't overdo your style risks, teachers will perceive your deviations as deliberate and not accidental. "

Chapter Sixteen:
Master High-Level Tricks

Tip for the Day: In honors English classes, AP and others, you will hear teachers speaking in what first may sound like foreign tongues. Without missing a beat, they refer to syllogisms, parallelism, nuances, and onomatopoeia. With your chin sinking lower, you wonder if it's too late for a schedule change. This garble sounds just as over-your-head as the stuff your IB math teacher talks about with equal flippancy. "We have the covalent blah-blah-blah over here, and existential algebra over there." You're pretty sure these teachers are way too smart for you, and that makes you eye the exit door with yearning.

Just before your mind goes into Titanic mode, relax. Think of what you know and what you don't know. By sophomore year in high school, you're familiar with metaphors, similes, and personification. You tackled those and made them yours, and now you will do the same thing with irony, satire, synthesis, and other dizzying terms. It may feel overwhelming at first, but soon, the differences will make writing essays more fun (in a weird English-class jargon kind of way).

The syllogism, for example, comes from the ancient Greek philosopher Aristotle, who saw syllogisms as essential tools for understanding knowledge by relying on simple declarative sentences and deductive reasoning. Basically, syllogisms help us categorize thoughts and reason logically. Let's refresh.

Syllogisms have a three-part structure: a major premise, a minor premise, and a conclusion. Your intention in using a syllogism is to figure out something.

Sample syllogism:

Major premise: All horses are mammals.

Minor premise: Seabiscuit is a horse.

Conclusion: Seabiscuit is a mammal.

Correct, right? This is a logical structure indeed, which makes "syllogism fallacies" the very unfortunate offshoots that lead to wrong conclusions.

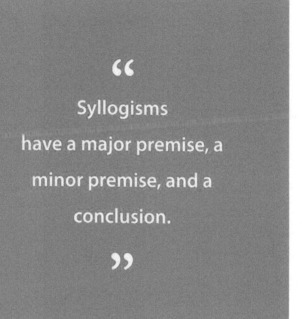

> "
> Syllogisms
> have a major premise, a
> minor premise, and a
> conclusion.
> "

Example:

Major premise: Poodles have curly hair.
Minor premise: Sabine Smith has curly hair.
Conclusion: Thus, Sabine Smith is a poodle.
No!

So, Was Aristotle Trying to Confuse Us?

In philosopher Aristotle's three books of his
treatise *Rhetoric*, he describes the three main methods

of persuasioin: logos, logical reasoning; ethos, character; and pathos, emotion ("Rhetoric," supersummary.com). Aristotle's point is that a speaker or writer who wants to persuade an audience can adopt a rhetorical style that appeals to a certain demographic. What's fascinating, is that even though Aristotle lived in a time when poetic language was cool, he discouraged it and instead recommended natural language and simple diction, probably because he realized that flowery language was a turnoff to most audiences ("Rhetoric"). People who write or speak in a condescending way come across as obnoxious. Therefore, when you write, it's better to be friendly. A slight degree of informality is all too underrated.

Other Nuances of Writing

Familiarity with certain terms helps you understand essay instructions as well as questions on SAT, ACT, and AP exams. Some of the terms here are ones that you probably *think* you know, but it never hurts to review them again.

Thesis sentence or statement: The basic argument a writer sets out to prove in an essay.

Topic sentence: The sentence that expresses the main idea of a paragraph.

Counterclaims: Essay views that differ from the argument the writer seeks to prove.

Contrarian: Views that are counter to the one a writer wants readers to accept.

Tone: An author's attitude toward subject matter.

Mood: The author's creation of a specific atmosphere meant to arouse certain emotions in readers.

Synthesis: A writer's way of combining ideas and finding multiple sources to make a specific point.

Bias: A writer's prejudice in favor of or against a person, group, or idea.

Point of view: A writer's position on an issue. Short form is POV.

Relevant: Adjective that means appropriate and important to the current time or circumstances.

Ambiguous: Adjective that means having a double meaning or open to more than one interpretation.

Irony: A literary technique, rhetorical device, or event that on the surface appears one way when in fact, it differs radically from what seems to be the case.

Figurative language: The phrasing that a writer uses to go beyond the literal meaning of a group of words or a word.

Simile: A figure of speech that compares two concepts by using "like" or "as." Examples: He is sly as a fox. She slept like a baby.

Metaphor: A figure of speech that compares two concepts but has no connecting words such as "like" and "as." It presents two separate things as if they were the same. Examples: She was a piece of work. He is a pacing lion. Sometimes, a writer uses what is called an "implied metaphor." This type isn't directly referenced. Example: "The coach barks at his basketball players until he is hoarse." The implied metaphor is that the coach is dog-like.

Personification: A writer speaks of an inanimate object, an animal, or weather as if it were a person. Examples: The wind howls. The fireplace danced embers into the room. The day crept by slowly.

Allusion: A writer refers to another text or person, place, or event. Examples: He was the Michael Jordan of fencing. The vacation spot was a total Shangri-La. From reading *The Old Man and the Sea*, by Ernest Hemingway, she learned about the pursuit of personal triumph.

Idiom: This is a turn of phrase that is not meant literally but used so commonly that everyone knows what it means. Examples: She paid through the nose for that pair of shoes. The understudy stole the star's thunder.

Pun: Typically humorous, a "play on words" takes advantage of a word's different meanings. Example: In the '80s, Houstonian Sherri Frank founded an aerobics studio called The Waist Basket, and people loved the "waste/waist" pun.

Onomatopoeia: "Buzz" and "drip" and "tick-tock" are words that sound like the things they describe. Poet Edgar Allan Poe was a master of onomatopoeia, with his "tapping, as of someone gently rapping, rapping at my chamber door" ("The Raven").

Assonance: Resemblance of sound in words or syllables. Example: "And so all the night-tide, I lie down by the side of my darling—my darling—my life and my bride" (repetition of the long "I" sound)—from "Annabelle Lee," a poem by Edgar Allan Poe.

Alliteration: This is a sound device occurring when words start with the same letter, such as "Peter Piper picked a peck of pickled peppers." Alliteration decorates language by building a mood, and thus, has a connection to figurative language.

Allegory: A story with a hidden moral or political meaning.

Parable: An earthly story with a heavenly meaning.

Fable: A short story with animal characters conveying a moral.

Symbolism: A writer's way of attaching meaning to a symbol, which can be an object or fact. For example, in Mark Twain's *Adventures of Huckleberry Finn*, the river represents freedom. In *Lord of the Flies*, the conch shell represents power. Offered on Hulu, the HBO series *Game of Thrones* uses the symbols winter and summer, as in "Winter is coming," the motto of House Stark, which is meant as a symbolic warning and a cry for constant vigilance ("Game of Thrones," HBO). Symbols can be colors, words, images, actions, or things.

Rogerian argument: The Rogerian argument, designed to convince or persuade, is argumentative reasoning that reaches a compromise by establishing middle ground between parties with opposing views. Human beings use this kind of argument in relationships; for example, if you want to watch a comedy and your sister is interested in a romantic film, why not try a romcom? The romantic comedy has both, and that makes it a good compromise.

Argument to convince: This relies on logic and evidence; a writer hopes to convince the readers that what he argues is true.

Argument to persuade: The persuasive argument depends on touching a person's emotions. The writer wants to persuade someone to believe or act a certain way.

Invitational argument: This argument invites participation in a conversation but does not seek to persuade. It means drawing a receiver of information into an open mind space but not trying to win the person over to another way of thinking.

Foreshadowing: In literature, foreshadowing signals what is to come in the story. An author might cue an upcoming weather catastrophe by having story animals act in peculiar ways, as if sensing trouble is imminent. An example from John Steinbeck's novel *Of Mice and Men,* is that the character Lennie likes to pet soft things like mice, which is the foreshadowing of tragedy.

Flashback: This is a commonly used device in a film or novel, when a scene "flashes back" to a time before the current plotline to add insights on the earlier period. An example would be Truman Capote's novel *In Cold Blood*, which has numerous flashbacks that give readers backgrounds of the characters, both the family members and the killers.

Satire: A writer uses humor, irony, exaggeration, and ridicule to spotlight ridiculous political issues, in particular. A classic example is author Jonathon Swift's famous satire, *A Modest Proposal.* Swift facetiously suggests that poor people should sell their children as dinners for the rich in order to lift the families out of poverty.

Connotation: The shades of meaning that a

word evokes from its use over the years. Example: The girl felt blue during the pandemic shutdown. Blue is a color, of course, but here, its connotation is sadness and depression.

Denotation: This is the dictionary definition of a word, and you can remember what it means because denotation and dictionary both start with 'd.'

Literal meaning: A reader takes a word at its most basic sense without any twists of metaphor. Example: Burton Folsom is braindead. Literally, this means the man has no brain function. However, if used figuratively, "braindead" means the writer thinks this man is acting stupidly. Also, there are instances when a person is being dramatic and says, "When he saw me without makeup, I wanted to die, literally and figuratively." Obviously, this is overstatement.

Figurative meaning: This refers to a word that is dressed up to amplify its meaning in a sentence. Example: She was bored stiff, not just bored. Example: The gym was as cold as a meat locker. Example: Agreeing to decorate the classroom, Elena went nuts (*figuratively*) with glitter.

Theme: This is the message that a story conveys. The theme of *One Hundred Years of Solitude*, by Gabriel Garcia Marquez, is isolation. The *Buendias* are solitary people living together as strangers in one house yet "disfigured 'forever and from the beginning of the world by the pox of solitude' that prevents communication with others" (Bell-Villada).

Speaking skills: The ability to articulate ideas.

Listening skills: The ability to listen and retain what was said.

Expository: Nonfiction text that gives facts and information about a topic.

Parallelism: A literary style that refers to a writer's arrangement of ideas in phrases, sentences, and paragraphs that balance one element with another of equal importance and similar wording. Example: I came, I saw, I conquered.

Parody: This is an exaggerated imitation of the style of a writer, artist, or genre in order to produce a comical effect.

Pastoral: Pastoral refers to a genre of literature, art, and music that depicts the shepherding lifestyle idealistically ("Pastoral," Wikipedia).

Juxtaposition: The act of placing two things together for the purpose of contrasting them. Example: "Ask not what your country can do for you; ask what you can do for your country," as President John F. Kennedy famously said.

Hyperbole: An exaggerated statement that is not meant to be taken literally. Examples: That pig is the fattest one in the universe. The teacher has a ton of papers to grade. Your parents are going to kill you when they hear what you did. That was the easiest quiz in the world. I'm dying of starvation. The room is freezing my toes off. Stop bothering me or I'm going to explode.

Attack *ad hominem:* Attack *ad hominem* comes from *ad hominem* (short for *argumentum ad hominem*), which refers to several arguments, some of which are fallacious (but not all). This term usually refers to a rhetorical strategy in which a speaker attacks a person (character, motive, or other attribute) rather than attacking the substance of the argument and thus avoids genuine debate by creating a diversion ("*Ad hominem,*" Wikipedia).

Trope: The use of a word or expression metaphorically or figuratively. Any literary device can be a trope. Common tropes are irony, metaphor, juxtaposition, and hyperbole. One of the most common TV tropes is "get rich quick." Numerous Netflix heist films have characters committing a crime to gain wealth, or it can be a family project-gone-wrong that is whimsical. In the Tom Cruise film *Jerry Maguire*, the famous catchphrase "show me the money" becomes a trope for fame and fortune. Another familiar trope is the impending threat factor in video games and suspense films. In a game, players keep facing off with bigger and better challenges or problems until they confront the most dangerous bad guy. A comical example of this trope is *Bridget Jones's Diary* star Renee Zellweger facing obstacle after obstacle on her road to finding true love; this trope is the reliable cornerstone of numerous romance novels, romcoms, etc.

Rhetorical question: This is a question asked for effect or to make a point, not to get an answer. Examples: "Are you kidding me?" "What am I doing here?" "Who knows?" "Is the pope Catholic?"

Understatement: A way of wording a comment so that something seems less important than it really is. Example: Looking at his ten shopping bags from Nordstrom, Albert's wife said, "I see you bought a couple of things today."

Overstatement: Exaggeration. A person expresses something too strongly. Example: "If I had wanted a banana, I would have ordered the entire Whole Foods produce department."

Antonomasia: A writer's substitution of an epithet or title for a proper name (king of rock 'n roll for Elvis Presley) or the use of a proper name that gives readers the point you are making. Example: "He was the Tom Brady of the corporate world." Or it can be slang, such as "teach" for an instructor, "guru" for a leader, "bigwig" for a CEO, or "playmaker" for a dealmaker's success or an athlete who puts a team in a position to score.

Anaphora: This is the deliberate repetition of a word or phrase at the beginning of a clause to achieve an artistic or poetic effect, such as, "It was the best of times, it was the worst of times," from Charles Dickens's *A Tale of Two Cities*.

Reversed structure: This refers to the way a writer reverses sentence structure from the normal subject-verb-object. (William Shakespeare often used this structure.)

Antithesis: A person or thing that is the direct opposite of something else. Example: Javier Bardem in the film *No Country for Old Men* is the antithesis of Julie Andrews in *Mary Poppins*. (He is devilish; she is angelic.)

Epitome: A person or thing that is a perfect example of something. Examples: Pop star Ariana Grande is the epitome of a small person with a powerhouse voice. A standard poodle is the epitome of a fancy show dog. A tsunami is the epitome of Mother Nature in tantrum mode.

Cliché: This is a tired, overused word or expression that signals a user's lack of original thought. Examples: Green as grass, black as coal, dark as night, mean as the devil, sweet as pie. Also, some words that have been used to the point of becoming clichés are: amazing, strategize, curated, awesome, disinformation, fake news, going forward, and mainstream media. Finally, and importantly, especially if you're Internet dating, beware of the word "entrepreneur" because all too often, a person referring to himself or herself as "entrepreneur" isn't one. The word is *almost* a synonym for "slacker piddling around on the Internet and pretending to be working." There are many exceptions, of course, but be wary of frauds.

What Are You DOING?

Want to increase your vocabulary or broaden your audience? Determine where you still want to go in essay writing. Undoubtedly, one goal is to write like a young person who is just a few years away from college or the corporate world. In both settings, people will expect you to have an extensive vocabulary that goes far beyond clichés.

Being able to write complete sentences should be a given. Keep in mind that in shooting for excellence, you must troubleshoot snags that get in the way of essay-writing success.

Review the following tips for assessing:

Always remember to read your teacher's instructions carefully. This is one spot where MANY students go wrong. For example, if your teacher says to write three paragraphs and the paper must be typed in 12-point font, Times New Roman, double-spaced, that's what she means as a BASIC requirement. If she asks you to embed at least three quotes and preferably more, that is a BASIC requirement. And if she tells you to write at least 400 words, that does not mean to write 200 or 1400. Simply following instructions will get you in a teacher's good graces faster than anything because it shows you are paying attention.

Ask for help when you need it. Teachers *want* to help you do well. Reach out. You *will* get assistance. The truth is, most teens do not understand how very eager teachers are to foster students' success. Liliana Rigdon, now a college sophomore but formerly a very proactive high school student, explains, "How can a teacher clear up confusion unless you ask? You don't have to be the top student in the class to profit from having a teacher provide clarification on any kind of assignment."

Rigdon's philosophy is that students waste time when they don't understand an assignment, but some remain reluctant to ask questions. Just email your teacher or tap on that shoulder and ask for an explanation; then you will be on the right path. It is impossible to write an excellent essay unless you comprehend the assignment.

Sometimes, too many instructions make you freeze up, but what will thaw your writing brain is having a teacher give you a "soft," to-the-point explanation of the direction where your essay should be headed. That untangles the instructions that boggle your mind.

Take each suggestion one by one. Don't let that fast-paced electronics brain of yours keep you from slowly parsing a set of instructions. An essay is not a quickie text. Slow down. Savor thoughts. Write in a deliberate, free-flowing way that is satisfying, but don't think in terms of finishing in two seconds by dashing out something.

Assess your understanding of key terms. Do you know *both* meanings of "voice"? Do you understand how to keep your essay in present tense, not past? Do you know how to supply TAG in the introduction? Are you putting GRAB, GAB, GLUE, GOODBYE into every essay?

Proofread carefully. Always reread an essay several times, and ask someone else to proofread it, too. You don't want typos to mar your final essay, and even writing pros sometimes read right over mistakes.

PART III:
Parent/Child Workshopping

Most moms and dads search for ways to help their children do well in school, and they are acutely aware of the importance of good writing. That's why the angle of Part III is letting parents in on a few ways they can make a difference in their children's education.

In all of these areas, the trick is intervening in a way that teens will listen, not bristle. Any parent of teens knows that this age bracket turns some kids into snarky, back-talking strangers, and that makes reaching them difficult, if not explosive. Do it right, though, and they will listen. Children sense when they are spinning out of control, and at such times, one of their deepest wishes is that someone would throw them a lifeline.

Chapter Seventeen:
Rev Up Motivation

Tip for the Day: In the classroom, adjustment issues are inevitable, and two are just regular issues of Electronics-Age childhoods—malaise and restlessness. Some children who weren't hyper before the pandemic now have trouble sitting still after spending so many hours on Zoom, tapping, texting, and electro-talking. And, in all fairness to Distance Learning, many schoolkids were already anxious pre-pandemic from overuse of electronics.

Motivation is what you need to succeed in the classroom, and the antidote to a lack of English-class motivation amounts to a simple recipe on how to write, what to write, what NOT to write. Teachers and parents can help you slap down those creepy naysayers in your head and turn out the kind of essays you envy.

Motivation Nation

With parents' and teachers' help, kids can rediscover the intrinsic motivation to learn. "Great teachers can inspire this in the classroom, but the influence of even the best teacher pales in comparison to that of a parent who's interested, invested, and involved," says Matt Armstrong, California AP and IB English teacher. "Parents need a how-to guide that explains how to assist their children on middle and high school writing assignments. We want to get parents sitting down with their kids and talking to them about their ideas and how best to express them."

Isabella Bottini, an American who currently teaches English in Madrid, Spain, says, "Motivation is a hard battle for some. However, my students who got behind during the pandemic put in lots of effort to catch up and made amazing progress. It was incredible to see their determination."

Referring to the year of Zoom studies, Marla Stewart, school counselor for grades 6 to 10, Federal Way Public Schools, Washington, says that older students suffered from being deprived of extracurricular activities (church, music lessons, theater, club sports and lessons, afterschool programs). Their lives revolved around "being connected to social media. These primary issues led to depression and anxiety."

Interestingly, Stewart saw elementary-aged kids bounce back socially and academically more quickly than secondary-aged kids. Most people thought it would be the opposite, which shows that the impact of Distance Learning is hard to measure.

Maria Otero, a middle-school counselor in the Federal Way Public School District in Federal Way, Washington, thinks Distance Learning affected many children dramatically. The cons were "being unengaged in classes, feeling unmotivated, and having no one to talk to about stressors." Otero also saw changes in sociability. "Some parents said that their kids wouldn't come out of their rooms." They no longer wanted to make friends or try new things.

Today, with kids back in classrooms, the entire spectrum of mental health issues comes to the forefront. Regarding motivation, author Melissa Mead calls it "a tricky thing" to discern who needs help in transitioning from home to classroom. "Problems are glaringly apparent in some kids while clues are subtle in others," notes Mead. From what she has observed thus far, classroom teaching requires both parents and teachers to collaborate on ways to help kids adapt successfully.

Concrete ideas are:

Focus on positives. Instead of warning that this or that will happen if they fail to deliver, tell your children or your students what will happen *when they do deliver.* Assume they will, and have rewards or recognition ready to go. "If children believe that they are safe and not many 'bad' things can happen, they are far more likely to stick their necks out and try," says Mead. "If they don't have to worry about repercussions, they are in a better mind place to deliver quality work than a rules-rigid setting that reminds kids at every turn that they must obey or else."

Give kids choices, even small ones, that increase their feeling of being in control. A teacher might ask if they want to do in-class essay writing on Mondays or Wednesdays, for example. Or would they prefer poetry or short stories for the month of November? Parents can ask their child if they want to do their homework right after school or wait until after dinner. Choices empower young people.

Clarify what they have to gain. When introducing a new "area" of study, teachers can tell students what they will aim for by listing learning objectives. Kids like goals because those are quantifiable "bull's-eyes" they can imagine.

Make classroom rules fair. The classroom atmosphere works best when teachers do not overwhelm students with so many guidelines and rubrics that it seems impossible to meet requirements.

Deal in positives. If a child asks about consequences, as in "What happens if I don't turn in my essay?" focus on your "faith" in them. Say: "I believe you want to succeed because I can tell you take pride in your work." In other words, don't announce the punishment phase unnecessarily. In fact, it may work best for a teacher to clarify that it seems unlikely any consequences for non-delivery will be necessary. "You're a hard-working, smart group of students." This is *always* a good approach, in home or school: operate on positives as a jumping-off point. Children try to meet good expectations just like they try to meet bad ones.

Show enthusiasm about teaching them and reading to them. If you're excited about the novel *The Book Thief,* by Markus Zusak, seeing your eyes flash with exclamation marks will ignite your students' interest.

Support teachers. Never, ever enter the forbidden territory of Teacher-Bashing/Blaming. No matter how you feel about a certain teacher, airing that

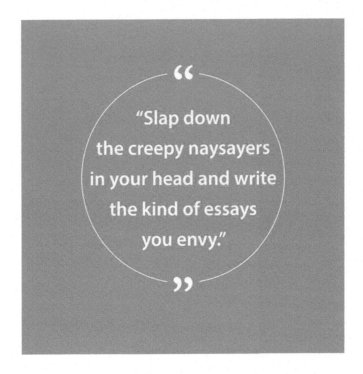

"Slap down the creepy naysayers in your head and write the kind of essays you envy."

grievance does not help your child, who inevitably feels caught in the middle. Children *want* to like their teachers, and some kids are even protective of them. Burst that bubble and you invite trouble. Instead, urge them to respect their teachers and forgive them when they make a mistake. When teachers, parents, and students team up, children benefit and deliver good work. For the child, harmony is a safe crucible in which success feels normal and doable.

Give kids chances to shine. Learn about likes and

dislikes, strengths and weaknesses, hobbies and sports, and highlight what they are good at doing. One of the best parenting tips I ever heard was this: *Constantly be on the lookout for chances to praise.* That attitude alone will generate good behavior. The way that encouragement inspires children is really remarkable. So, when you "catch" your child doing even the slightest "positive" action, heap on the praise. That motivates kids to keep doing the things that elicit compliments and thus experience good feelings like the last time. By the same token, *don't overplay mistakes.* If you put a huge emphasis on screwups, you will see Incredible Shrinking Egos. Remember the boss you had who beat you up with your deficiencies until your desire to please changed to anger and then indifference? The child who gets battered verbally soon will *just not care* or will accept the newly defined persona that you assigned him—as a loser kid who can't get anything right.

Bottom line: point out an error, ask for improvement, and move past a behavior lapse ASAP. You are saying, for children's ears, *it is my job to help you shape up, but that won't take much time because you're already such an excellent kid.* It's a no-fail approach to child-rearing and child-teaching; accentuate the positive and minimize the negative.

Go places. Take field trips and zoo trips. Explore

parks and beaches. Check out books at the library. Stage a book fair. Try offbeat learning modes to engage curiosity. Read to your kids, no matter how old they are. Read to your students, no matter how old they are.

Grow self-esteem. Help children feel like valued members of the school community by appointing them to different classroom posts. Have one of them hand out computers. Ask someone else to come up with a "Thought for the Day." This works at home, too. The more your child contributes, the greater his confidence.

Ask kids who like to mentor to serve as classroom "peer tutors." You can announce that when Kyle needs help with his math, Mateo is going to provide it. Similarly, when Samantha gets stuck when writing an essay, Jill will be the one to guide her.

Balance group work carefully. When it's team project time, all too often the high achievers end up doing the heavy lifting while the slackers bask in the sun and sip pink-umbrella drinks. Match kids with similar work ethics to come up with equitable group projects that don't end in tears, recriminations, and parent emails. Also, ask students for their ideas on ways to make teamwork more efficient and fairer.

Hold out "carrots" that make kids want to get involved. Read examples of good essays. Walk around the classroom and look for excellent introductions that you, as teacher, can enthuse over with kudos-to-the-moon-and-back. Announce to the class that you're searching for a very unique simile or metaphor, and if you spot one, that kid wins an instant A.

Help children learn to self-praise, self-study, and self-evaluate. If your straight-A son makes his first ever C on a report card, ask him how *he* feels about it. Truthfully, how you feel is kind of irrelevant in regard to change-making. Only when children get in charge of their own academic destinies does it benefit them long-term. Meanwhile, they like riding on parents' and teachers' coattails, where bailing is always an option. Tell children they can climb to any level academically if they are willing to expend the time and study required.

Handle underachievers carefully. Teachers and parents are wise to accept that there are always going to be kids (yours and other people's) who *just do not care* about grades or school. These children understand, in general, that they need math and English, for example, but excelling on writing a rhetorical essay is not on their radar screen and never will be. However, you can help them become successful people by tracking their interests and encouraging them to do well in those.

My brother loved making birdhouses and

treehouses, but at school, he often stared out the window at the great outdoors. No amount of trickery changed his course, and my parents tried the whole gamut of rewards. However, he did become a successful builder even though he never once set his sights on being a star student. When our parents saw that he wanted to be a star *person*, though, they encouraged the fire he had in him for building. That made his confidence soar; no one made him feel that he had to be Mr. Academia. Adults fostered his growth and helped him enjoy being the guy he was, in a field that made him happy. What better recipe for life success?

Don't compare siblings or students. Pounce on what kids do well, and praise generously. Don't tell them how they are disappointing you. Build them up, love who they are, and your children will find their way. Witness any high school junior gritting her teeth as she studies for upcoming SATs, and you will walk away quite certain that nothing in the world is worth that kind of anxiety. Overemphasis on performance in children does not seem to be creating many happy adults.

- Let their grades be *their* grades.
- Let their hobbies be *their* choices.
- Let their career aspirations be ones *they* discovered.

The more you equip children for driving themselves places, the faster they will become citizens of the world with voices of value. That doesn't mean life won't crash their dreams or rewrite their script, but it does mean that no matter what their fate, they will have within them the wherewithal to cope. (What is wherewithal? *Resources and strength.*) If you believe that you can do something and have the right stuff in your backpack, you usually can pull it off.

Chapter Eighteen:
Manage Teen Anxiety

Tip for the Day: Daily use of electronics often leads to ADHD symptoms, so it's a good idea to watch for signs in your children and in you. Some red flags include: inability to focus, difficulty sitting still, and a tendency to thrash from one task to another.

Cell phones. Anxiety. ADHD. Sketchy images. Are we multitasking kids into early graves or are devices simply inevitable parts of today's culture? Breaking down each of these areas, we give you, the parent or teacher, some handy advice on managing the many facets of living in an electronics age. From anxiety induced by social media comparisons to

ADHD symptoms that cell phones spawn, there are numerous issues that adults must deal with effectively to help kids leap over the hurdles they face.

Especially alarming to many parents are the twitches and restlessness that many youngsters exhibit. School psychologists and teachers see these problems increasing in number. Thus, if you spot "electronics heebie-jeebies," it is important to address the problem and provide coping mechanisms. Devices aren't going away, nor should they be banned from use, mainly because turning cell phones into forbidden fruit just makes them ten times more attractive than they were before you became the Electronics Police.

Too much tech *cannot* cause ADHD. Even though ADHD-like symptoms concern adults, Michael Manos, Ph.D., of The Cleveland Clinic, says that too much tech does not give birth to this disorder ("Can Too Much Tech..?" and "Understanding Nuances"). At the same time, though, excessive gaming and posting on Facebook are problematic when such activities cause symptoms similar to those seen in children with ADHD.

Most teachers can attest that high school students who use digital media several times a day frequently are inattentive; they may have difficulty organizing and completing tasks, exhibit hyperactivity and impulsivity, and almost always have trouble sitting still.

ADHD, of course, is a genetic disposition characterized by hyperactive and impulsive behaviors involving physical changes in the brain. Using digital media can create symptoms that resemble ADHD ("Can Too Much Tech....?").

Electronic pastimes can sap a person's attention. Young people, in particular, are conditioned to listen for every time their phones beep or they get an email, text, or notifications. Naturally, they want to respond.

To reset a child's responses for greater success in school, parents can teach their children how to prioritize *consciously*. Having a phone set on silent to respect school rules isn't nearly enough; a phone still demands attention when it buzzes because it's hard for kids to resist taking a quick peek. Furthermore, phones are good at grabbing attention because alerts, notifications, and ads are designed to stimulate, making it hard for teens to focus on assignments.

What's the best answer for antsy kids? Parents and teachers can encourage teens to make a conscious choice not to let devices run their lives. Endorse the idea of being proactive and taking charge. Kids may respond favorably because many teens flourish when teachers or parents signal that they believe in them. Convey a "life management" approach by sharing that anyone is better off making personal decisions on time management, and no one should let an anonymous Silicon Valley CEO dictate lifestyle choices. When teens decide how their time is spent, they can prevent texting and posting from consuming all their spare time and ruining their GPA.

How to Compartmentalize and Like It

Agile tapping fingers remind parents that kids learn in unprecedented ways. News blasts them hard and fast, early and often, which results in super-short attention spans. This makes it extremely important for kids to learn how to handle distractions. One workable idea is rewarding teens for *planning* their accessibility to those who text and summon them.

Actually, a notification sound is only a "bid" for attention, so just because a text arrives does not mean you have to abandon what you're doing and race to respond. Other parts of life matter, too. Ask your teen to come up with a plan for compartmentalizing electronics responses so that move can keep him or her from becoming Pavlov's[4] dog.

If your child is reluctant, set up rules to limit time spent on devices.

---

[4] Pavlov's dog refers to a scientific experiment to show a conditioned response to a bell that made dogs salivate. When food was no longer given, the dogs still salivated at the bell.

Suggest, for example, that your children designate an hour or two in the evening for posting on social media and texting friends. If you can get them to try putting things in compartments, you're handing them a good skill for moderation. Point out that a life of overlapping electronics leads to the sad state of parents texting while their children are trying to talk with them. *Bad manners.* When do we call this out for what it actually is?

The message: Be respectful of those who are talking with you, and, in turn, you can expect them to listen with uninterrupted attention. Have family times that exclude electronics. Maybe try the "corporate meeting plan" of dropping phones in a box by the door and picking them up again after dinner or after the meeting or after class.

Learning to allot time for different things in a day inevitably leads to better grades. Also, when your teen talks about wanting a better report card, suggest altering his environment by reining in impulses that make him give in to distractions.

Recommend ideas emphatically. *This is important stuff.* Also, remind the young that they do not get a second chance to make a first impression with teachers. "Make them remember you as a bright, engaged learner, not a half-checked-out zombie."

It is necessary for children to learn how to move

from fun rides (gaming) to real-life commutes. Although electronics addictions are natural offshoots of our multi-buzzing lives, we can also teach young people how to keep "toys" from running their lives.

Accept Help

After a year-and-a-half of Distance Learning, it may have taken teens some time to adjust to teachers' presence. Remember, though, that teachers care. They are smart. They want their students to succeed.

What really helps teens reorient is having parents offer pointers for curbing instant-gratification instincts. Ask children to set aside times for doing things *beyond* electronics. Model it. Point out how you do it. Promise teens that prioritizing activities will change their lives in a good way. You may be surprised to find that they will accept guidance cheerfully (probably because they are worried themselves about the time electronics consume).

30 Minutes, One and Done!

When a teacher assigns an essay that requires slowing down, teens may experience anxiety associated with the blank screen or blank pages. Problem is, most teens instinctively want to be able to write an essay as quickly as they answer a text: bang, zip, and done. When this doesn't happen, they feel bummed and assume that essays will be "no fun."

The secret, then, is reframing the essay-writing gig. ***Turn this into a time for reflection and peaceful thoughts.*** The essay getaway can become something teens can anticipate. Safe and secure from the world's chaos, a teen moves into a calming mind refuge perfect for renewal of thoughts, plans, ideas.

The Internet and its sidekick devices have opened the door to unprecedented ways of doing research and growing intellectually, not to mention playing games. Thus, Generation Z kids have the potential to be the smartest generation ever. The key is accepting that not everything has to be click, swipe, fast-fast. When they make a free-will choice to observe a slow-down, they can use their newly developed essay skills to write thoughtfully. Also, this teaches teens to stop cell-phone-checking from taking over and usurping family time, sports, and other quality moments. *Be your own boss*—that's the message.

Ideally, children will find time for everything. Believe it or not, even they suspect (secretly) that electronics should not be pervasive in every part of their lives. Why not remind them that doing homework and chores before using devices is a good order of priorities?

Also, hearing parents mention their own desire

for "Me Time" helps kids feel less alone.

You may even encourage your child (or your students) to set up a weekly calendar in which they set aside times for electronics checking/posting, homework, family time, sports, etc. Living randomly is not a viable approach for success in life. One Colorado dad says, "I think telling kids that they can prioritize games over homework is a losing battle that gives them a good excuse for not getting essays done on time." In other words, providing guidelines is beneficial and does not have to evolve into a parent-as-dictator standoff. Kids often become reasonable when parents are reasonable.

Think of the support that teens will need in order to handle college days with post-COVID electronics addictions still going full blast. The average college freshman *must* be able to say, "I can do some gaming from 9-11 at night, but I have to save earlier hours in the day for classes, socializing, meals, and studies." Otherwise, a kid who lets gaming or posting or texting dominate waking hours, will struggle in school.

As a parent, your decision to hand over some "tools" for solving this dilemma is as important as teaching a kid to use an ATM, manage money, and do homework. Don't expect compartmentalization to happen by osmosis or just because your teen *needs* to develop this skill. Some adult-in-charge must lead a teen toward making good choices in life's important "curriculum" as well as the cafeteria line.

Getting behind the eight-ball in high school or college is a daunting experience, but it is also one that parents can help a young person avoid. If you get nothing but eye-rolling resistance when you suggest allocating times for electronics, studies, etc., then ask your teen to offer his or her thoughts on solving the problem. While some children can benefit from a session or two with a guidance counselor who specializes in time management, what's ideal is having a parent set the standard. When you model good use of time, that speaks more loudly than anything. (Obviously, teens will be amused by a parent who insists on time allocation but is infamous for checking her or his cell phone 150 times a day.)

Getting Real

The Internet has endless wonders that tug at our attention. However, it is smart for all of us to understand that the cyber-world is "ad-driven." That makes us less likely to bow to every directive that provocative apps announce. Being manipulated is not ideal. Decide your own path and preferences.

Remind your child that a phone's provocative buzz does not really need an immediate response. Ask

your teen if he or she can imagine ending electronics'
dominance over every hour of the day. You can
decide not to let others call the shots. Some teens and
adults declare 5 to 6 p.m. as their catch-all time slot
for checking phone messages, and that allows them to
be fully attentive during all of their daytime in-person
encounters.

In addition, children will feel more in charge if
they allot sufficient time to grasp the basics of writing
good essays. As early chapters of *Epic Essays* explain,
the four Gs will fuel essay writers for hitting the road
locked-and-loaded, ready to write.

On a regular basis, gently encourage your kids to
focus. Point out that they will have hours afterward to
answer texts, DMs, emails, and rejoin multiplayer
gaming partners. Who knows? You may get your
teens so inspired about this new day/new way that
they actually sit down for dinner with the family—and
say things.

In some homes, family dinner still is a
requirement; in many, it has gone out of style. My
father always tried to persuade young parents that a
together dinner was a bedrock institution of a strong
family because it encourages communication. My
parents and I talked current events, activities, and my
brother would propose his latest crazy VW van
junket; however, what I remember most is that my

parents made us feel that we had a voice; they would hear us out, no matter how outrageous our ideas or plans. That was why dinnertime became a uniting factor at our house. The push-pull of outside demands, work, and friends faded away for an hour, and we looked each other in the eye and spoke in full sentences.

Of course, parents today face more hysterical times, with parents and kids constantly dashing out the door for sports practice or orchestra rehearsal or PTA meetings or Pilates class. Still, when you, the "modeling parent," discuss compartmentalizing, why not suggest that they (and you) pencil in a few family dinners just to see how the bonding improves? Experimentation never hurts.

Lend Me Your Ear

Now for the elephant in the room. By the time they reach teen years, many kids go through a Black Angst Phase in which they doubt their parents' intelligence. (My parents aren't cool, so how can they be smart?) Overnight, teen hubris turns your little darlings into jaded cynics. Many admit that they don't think there is much to learn from discussions with family.

If only they knew! Even Old Granddaddy can offer fascinating tales, and who knows when it might be the teens' last chance to hear them? I've heard many people express regrets that they somehow never learned much about their parents.

Maybe you should point out: Did you know Great-Granddad fought in the Vietnam War and would love to tell you about it? Did you know Grandma was the first student to speak on women's rights on a college campus right after giving a book report on *The Feminine Mystique*? Also, parents and grandparents can share stories about their childhoods as long as they leave out the "life was so much better back then." Gen Z kids are lugging around enough baggage, and the last thing they need is to feel like they're growing up in the worst imaginable era. In truth, every generation's childhood has pros and cons, and these electronics kids will have their own stories to tell someday.

Multi-Not So Much

The young person who sits in front of the computer, multiple screens in play, gaming, homework, team assignment, does feel in charge of things, but it's only a façade. Why? Successful multitasking is a myth. Most teens say they are

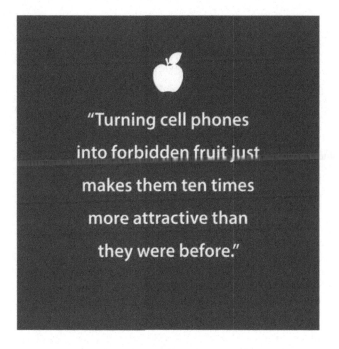

"Turning cell phones into forbidden fruit just makes them ten times more attractive than they were before."

masters of it, but research proves what actually happens; in reality, teens skim the surface when handling several tasks simultaneously. Then, when tested, the information they *barely* learned is not there for recall because they just glided past it rather than absorbing it. Then they still wonder why they failed.

Good writers and readers focus. Do you want to submit an essay that reflects well on you—or are you satisfied with work that is so nonsensical even you can't remember what you meant when you wrote it? Really, the sooner teens realize they are giving

everything short shrift by multitasking, the better.
Change the tasking to a one-at-a-time pursuit.

Self-Monitoring Internet Images

Face it. You, a teen, must learn how to tame the quick-draw fingers that get you in trouble on social media and on your cell phone. Online images are important, and kids already know by the end of fifth grade that their words become "permanent" in texts, social media posts, and emails. Every year, teachers and parents remind them hundreds of times.

Mention the "rules" and watch them roll their eyes. Even so, the scare tactics did not stick. Feeling impervious to normal hazards, thousands of teens fire off hasty messages and end up regretting things they let fly into the Cloud. This shouldn't surprise elders because kids through the ages have always been notorious for failing to reflect before speaking or writing. They blurt out what they think, and today's platforms are numerous, limitless, and loud.

Help your children. Encourage them to get out of the noisy fast lane of cyber communications and swerve over to a quiet park for essay writing. Tell them you know this will feel different from charged-up texting, but ask them *just to consider* the possibility that thoughtful times might be refreshing.

Also, while you're at it, encourage teens to stay

"classy" in pictures and words they post. Just because their peers blast obscenities online does not make that a fabulous idea. Even though teens have heard it before, remind them that a prospective employer or college admission counselor may choose to review social media posts just to get a feel for personalities and reputations. Teens who like to shock with sketchy images, talk of drug use, and/or vicious chatter will wind up sorry they were impulsive. Words and photos can and do come back to haunt, and once the mistake is made, it is hard to get the images corrected or deleted.

As you offer tips, communicate without making teens feel "spied on." And if you don't believe in coddling because you're the household "boss," remember that actually reaching their ears and having information permeate defensiveness is the goal, and this will always be challenging. Never hurts to sample fresh ways of getting through iron walls.

Even kids who need guidance won't have open arms just because they need help. Distancing occurs in teen years as a very normal part of breaking the last shreds of that umbilical cord. Teens often think that they can't wait to be adults at long last *so no one can tell them what to do*, but a deficit of skills makes this a precarious journey. A little hand-holding never hurts.

Every teen feels old enough and tall enough and

mature enough to make decisions. However, does your child know what to do about a problem like anxiety? Furthermore, when he or she last screwed up on social media, did they know how to evaluate the damage done and push a reset button? Is your child able to get over a heartbreak without cratering into some dark domain?

Encourage your teen to sort thoughts and decide which ones are ready for prime time and guard online first impressions. Having a "forked tongue" might come in handy as a writer at times, but it will do a teen no favors in regard to friendships if he or she peppers people with vitriol online. When a young person gets confused about what to share with others, a parent can communicate a readiness to talk and listen without judgments.

Take every opportunity to share with your child that teen years are only *a tiny slice* of their lives. Assure them, "There is so much more ahead, and you'll be better equipped with experience. Give yourself a break!"

From time immemorial, teens have supersized their disappointments, but today's cyber environment makes things scarier because of the abundance of tragic online stories about kids ending their own lives. There is no doubt this contributes to the likelihood of 'normal kids' pondering suicide. Parental intervention, though, can be lifesaving. In other words, it is wise to keep a close eye on your child after a breakup or a letdown at school, and be ready to point to the long haul of lives and the many future opportunities for happiness and success. That will help your teen put disappointments in perspective. While your son may be convinced that there will never be another girl like the one who just ended a relationship with him, the truth is that he will have other "possibilities." Life is long, and there are many people to befriend.

Supersizing Every Crisis

With the rise in teen suicide today, both parents and teachers need to understand what inspires suicidal ideation in young people. In handling this cataclysmic problem, one area for examination is the adolescent tendency to supersize problems. It's an actual fact that the classic "breakup" feels bigger, more horrible, and is more potentially life-threatening at age sixteen than it is at age thirty.

What you, as a parent or teacher, can do to help young people in despair is to help them "reframe" a rough situation. In talks with the young, wear the "positivity hat" but also sound realistic. No one's judgment at age sixteen is perfect, no matter how good their grades. Maturity and intelligence are different things.

Bottom line, encourage a disappointed kid (let's call her Matilda) to accept some "babying" from you, the parent, especially that day when a buddy since kindergarten decides to kick their long-term friendship to the curb. Worse, the other girl's mom reads some texts that Matilda sent, decides that she's a bad influence. In a single day, Matilda's world comes tumbling down, thanks to electronics.

How does someone survive heart-crushing moments? Many people can show they care: Parents. Friends. Teachers. Aunts. Uncles. Each adult in a teen's inner circle has experienced letdowns, and that means he or she can provide *valuable insight* to help a young person. Those times when life is outrageously cruel, every teen *does need* a sympathetic person close by. Just avoid saying "That's not such a big thing" or "Who cares if he doesn't like you anymore?" Never minimize what someone else considers a major deal. It *is* big to your child; that much is clear, and in such instances, the teen's perception is all that matters.

Tip for teens: *It is okay to vent and complain. Cry. Throw stuffed animals. Then, if you're lucky, maybe your mom will take you shopping and buy you a lift-the-spirits gift. In a few days, the world will feel friendlier, and although you may remain disappointed, the truth is, your ex best friend is not the only person in the world who can be your confidante.*

Try to learn from letdowns. Think before you post or text. Is this something that could come back to hurt me? Or is it worded so that no one will be offended? Does it show my best or worst self? Do I really need to say this?

Never in history has it been so easy for teens to write toxic comments that hundreds of eyes can read. This era graphically teaches the lesson that *you don't need to say everything you feel.* Just because you're experiencing strong feelings doesn't mean you should air them. Rein in your blast-the-world instinct. Not everyone has to hear your every thought.

Chapter Nineteen:
Publish, Young or Old

Inquisitive people who want to write are thirsting to find the Writing Well. How do you stick your pail in and withdraw skills? Common questions:

1. How do you know what to write?
2. Where does it come from?
3. How do you get published?

Most friends and readers ask me about getting agents or publishing stories and articles and books. Over the years, I've amassed many tips. It's just like slopping Horizon organic skim milk and Tazo Skinny Chai Latte into a saucepan, turning on the burner under it, sitting down at my computer, and only remembering it when I hear the liquid spitting "Hey, I'm boiling over here!" Reminders, I *need* them. So, I keep working on pass-it-on stuff (this book).

Truly, I want to inspire people to write simply because it is fulfilling. It's there—like mountains that tempt climbers. More than anything, writing can be a comforting pastime that lets you commit thoughts to paper (or computer) and then look at them after they chill for a while, and you can view them with objectivity. Is this anything I want to keep? Is it a thought I want to expand on?

That First Sale!

Best idea ever for wannabe authors: Design an article or story to fit a specific venue and make it exactly the kind of thing that magazine or website is buying. I read that in *Writer's Digest* when I first began freelance writing, and I can promise you that tip leads to a sale faster than anything. Most writers pen a random piece on knitting needles and then waste months trying to peddle it to the wrong magazines.

Do your homework on places to publish that actually buy freelance stories and articles. Nothing will move your goal forward more quickly. If you submit a short story to a publisher that says clearly on its website that it accepts no fiction, what *are* you doing?

All too often, writers, operating from a bizarre strain of hubris, cultivate certainty that their story or novel or article will knock down the walls of a

"For fiction, keep your mind and heart open to see how your characters develop."

publishing house; overnight, the editors will change their entire thrust. Sad to say, that rarely happens. Most have sets of editorial guidelines they adhere to simply because they know what their readers want and do not deviate from delivering exactly that.

It doesn't hurt to write what you want to write but be smart when you set out to find a home for it. A literary agent makes the book-manuscript-selling process move faster, but it is almost as hard to locate an agent to represent you as it is to find a receptive publisher. In today's fast-changing world of publishing, the walls are extremely high, which leads you to opt for patience or self-publishing. Agents typically don't sell articles simply because these are easy for writers to sell; plus, the money is too little to justify the time they would invest.

Both self-selling and agent-selling have advantages. If you choose to self-publish, be sure to read publishing guru Jane Friedman's amazing analysis of options. She has the gospel, from hybrid publishing to the ups and downs of Amazon. It's all in blog after blog (https://www.janefriedman.com). If you choose to wait for a publisher to notice your book, it may take more time than you expected, but that doesn't matter unless your book has a time element to it. If it is timely, self-publish and chances are good that if it touches a chord (and hasn't been done to death), people will find it.

Listen. Look. Write. Snack.

Whatever you choose to write, find a topic that makes you smile. Summertime? Gaming? Shih-tzus? Rerun your years so far. What was a moment that you managed something special and maybe people noticed or maybe you wish they had? Narrate your early years the way you remember them. Or write fiction "based on" your childhood.

Let's say you want to write about three people (always the best idea for fiction). Think of characters in books you've loved. Who was your favorite character in the last book you read and why—or your most-loved Netflix show? Now grab a writing pad or laptop and go to the mall or the park. Sit on a bench and describe people you observe—write down thoughts.

A Sample "Day at Park" Story

Maybe you see two nannies chatting while their kiddos-in-strollers drool. Let's call her Mimi, the shorter of the two, who has a habit of giggling before the other person speaks, and each time she does, a lot of nodding goes on, as if she is encouraging the other woman to talk. Mimi is round-bodied like a ripe pear, her face a valentine, her lips plump and pleasant—and she is very blink-blink-blinky. The other person has a long neck, long eyelashes, and long legs. Thin in a modelish way, she looks like her name would be Elle or Es—and the beauty of her face takes your breath away. Elle's ruling trait that you notice first is that she bites her bottom lip on one side when she's tense. Not often but it's there, subtle—and kind of touching in a drop-dead gorgeous female. You sense that these women are discussing men; little else could cause such a range of expressions—worried, thrilled, and self-conscious. Little Mimi is the one giving advice; Elle is inhaling it in that odd way that some people have of barely acknowledging that she is being tutored. Suddenly, Elle shifts gears and stands up. "You know nothing about me," she says in a voice so loud you can hear her. "I'm happy when I'm with Tristan— *most* of the time."

"Except when you're not," says Mimi with an eye-roll. "Hey, love isn't supposed to make you cry."

Elle crosses her arms over her chest and ducks her chin so low it grazes the neck of her zipped-up red velveteen hoodie. "All my relationships make me cry," she says.

"Dr. Phil says, 'you teach people how to treat you,' and I really believe that."

"What does that even mean?"

Mimi shakes her head. "It means if you let someone tromp all over you, you get more of the same. But reject abuse, and the guy shapes up or ships out."

Elle cringes. "Yeah, and I'm afraid of the shipping-out part."

"Hon, if you lose someone who's making you sad, what have you lost?"

Elle sits down, hugs herself, rocks on the bench. She does not make eye contact. It's like a little beetle pulling its head into the shell. Not a word.

Mimi moves over, puts her arms around Elle's shoulder. "What do I know?" Mimi says. "I've never even had a long-term boyfriend." The unsaid message: she sets high standards.

Elle hikes up her head, the long neck now a posture asset. Then she reverts to the lip-bite. She digs the toe of her Adidas Superstar sneaker in the sand in front of the wooden bench.

"I'm such a loser," Elle says.

"No, you're not." Mimi slumps lower and lets her long brown hair drape over the back of the bench. "But, sis, you can't marry a bad boy."

Elle taps all of her fingers on her lips like a pianist prancing on black and white keys.

Character tags are the little trademarks that separate characters so your readers can keep them straight. Give each of the three below a significant tag that will help anyone reading your story keep the characters straight:

Annabelle: Bugs her eyes when she gets excited about what she's saying.

John-Paul: Picks his teeth with a toothpick, always has one hanging on his lips.

Adrianna: Laughing eyes say she has never met a hurdle that got her down.

Character Whirlwind

Not every single character has to be gorgeous or brilliant or even entertaining. The world is full of people who, in a story, would be primarily "placeholders." They fill roles as narrators or equalizers or friend-counselors. Also, don't give facsimiles of real-life people their real-life names or you'll get sued! Instead, rename them, and mix up the traits in different characters. Don't make your protagonist an exact replica of someone you know. It's not fair or smart.

Keep your mind and heart open to see how characters develop. Recall your days playing with a dollhouse when you could easily determine which lunatics were running the asylum. You made the daughter-in-the-pink-dress a piece of work, always bossy and sure to give everyone in the family headaches. The brother, Fletch, was a smiling peacemaker; he soothed ruffled feathers all the livelong day with his easygoing personality. Curly-haired Mother, dressed in ruby red, was a gentle spirit who ran the house like General Patton; she looked benign but was really a force that parted waters, and no one did anything naughty when she was around. Dad in the gray suit was a laughing, back-slapping man, who took his kids on secret trips to Jolly Cone for ice cream and handed them the car keys (behind

Mom's back) before they knew how to drive.

Never ignore where a cast of characters is taking you. If you have a good ear, you will be able to sense what they would say and want and what moves they would take. Bring them alive by allowing them to bloom, just like you would if you were a parent. Don't stuff them with your own traits.

Each person is different in eccentricities, and writing lets you explore that truth. Unearth characters so interesting you'll wish you could take them with you on a trip to Vegas. Make them lively, complex, and flawed (but not so flawed they have no redeeming characteristics at all). Think actor Billy Bob Thornton. He is an extremely appealing character in *Goliath* because he is smart, loyal-to-friends, and peppered with idiosyncrasies.

Do not write fiction that *lacks* a hero/heroine. Everyone hates wasting time on a film that signals from the start that there is no one to root for; the story is peopled with villains, rogues, and ne'er-do-wells, yet you foolishly keep watching and later wind up wishing you could get back those two lost hours of your life.

That is what you don't want to happen with your writing. For example, no matter how irredeemable the evil dirtbags in Truman Capote's novel *In Cold Blood*, the reader has to find out what happens to them because they become flesh and blood—on paper. Masterful Capote makes these bad guys so intriguing the reader has to get to know them. No one leaves that book half-read.

In nonfiction, show your humanity. Think of your reader as a friend. Also, in fiction, be sure to make some characters charming (what's not to like about your creations?). That helps you enjoy spending months or years with them.

Come on Along—Plot or Thesis

Whether you create characters (for a story) or your own thoughts (essay), keep in mind that you will start with a hint (GRAB) in the first paragraph, by saying here's:

- What you want to prove
- What you hope to persuade readers to believe
- What kind of a trip they will go on with you— thriller, romance, or science fiction.

A reader who loves suspense will hate investing time in a romcom if that's a genre that person isn't into; no one wants to find out the bad news 50 pages into reading. Think of a magazine article you have read that gets you going (interest-wise) in three paragraphs. Think of a story you've read that hooks you from page one. Try to mimic the way the author writes. Make the beginning your best writing, for example. Do several drafts. After you write, leave the introduction alone for a day and then review it. If it doesn't excite you, keep rewriting until it thrills you *at least* a smidge.

Also, check for clarity. Can your reader tell what-the-heck you're talking about and where you're headed with this beginning? Are you identifying the people you mention?

Write a little anecdote. Here's what happened to you or to someone. And drive home the point or lesson learned. Then head down the plot or essay trail with a "climax" or argument in mind. You have a destination although it may feel like rambling because you are picking up on clues as you go. This can alter your stance, and that's okay. Don't freeze your writing in time. Instead, be alert to nuances: shapes of clouds, sounds of growls, ferocity of winds, and smells of Dumpsters.

Keep a journal. Doodled words are easy to lose, but you can always use "Notes" in your cell phone. Take advantage of those feelers of yours; have them out at all times so that nothing gets past you. Before it does, jot it down.

Try this plan for a story:

- Grab with a stunning statement that puts your reader in the middle of the action.
- Roll out the idea.

- Explain what came before (background) in *a few* sentences (for clarity).
- Pull readers into the party.
- Tip the writing to hit a high point (your climax gob-smack or thesis ta-dah).
- End with a few final throws of glitter or fairy dust.
- Savor what you wrote. Pat yourself on the back for the "good stuff."
- Tie up loose ends with a sentence telling why your point matters!
- Mess around. Shuffle ideas. Experiment. See what works.

Tweak Set-in-Stone Ideas about Writing

Keep in mind, as you write, that people mainly hear only the things they want to hear. Try to listen well. Absorb critiques. Be the unusually intuitive person who takes in every tip. If your English teacher says you need to read lots of books, do exactly that; start reading more. How do you react?

- **Your writing instructor says you "overwrite."** So, use less gunk. Pay attention to that the next time you write. Pare it down.
- **Your mother says she doesn't understand the first two pages of your essay.** Instead of

losing your temper and screaming that she knows nothing, ask what isn't clear. Did you mention a person without saying what kind of authority he is, position or credentials? Did you refer to a period in history that isn't generally known and needs to be defined? Say, you write that Maximilian Bryan thinks author Tim O'Brien, author of *The Things They Carried*, is a true craftsman of characterization; then your reader asks, who the heck is Maximilian Bryan? A book critic? President of the PTA? CEO of Lens-o-Plenty? Define people you quote; otherwise, you risk losing your readers the second they get confused.

- **Your best friend says that your writing "flat-lines."** Don't un-Friend him. Instead, add more hills and valleys. Vary sentence lengths. Be descriptive—add metaphors, similes, and personification.

- **Your brother says he got bored reading the first page.** Don't hang up on him. Spice up the ingredients so your reader feels worried, scared, sad, or mad. Just don't let your writing be melatonin.

Why listen to critics? The reality is, you make faster progress when someone calls you out for parts that don't work. Especially, *please-please-please* consider remarks that you hear several times. This is like paying attention when your wife complains that you're boastful. An annoying trait, so why not work on it? She said it. Your best friend said it. Your mom said it. Work on it and see how that turns out. Why keep making the same mistakes over and over? When someone critiques your writing, do not shoot back with a defensive remark ("Yeah, like *you* know so much"). Also, do not make it your mission in life to ensure that everyone knows what's what. That is a downside of writers; we have read so much, so widely, that we do know a lot of "stuff," and many of us love to regale people with truckloads of knowledge and continually set the record straight. But don't. Instead, take that trivia you've accumulated and go on "Jeopardy." There, someone will appreciate that fund of information, and you'll even win money.

All Those Books You Abandoned

Readers get bored fast. Divide them into two categories: Those who will read a few pages of a book they buy and then bail. And those who will finish any book just because they paid "good money" for it (martyrs and masochists). They want to be able to declare that they never, ever fail to complete a book. In their minds, there is some pie-in-the-sky trophy for grueling reading longevity. There isn't, of course, but don't tell them.

Anyway, all you have to do is plop out your gut beliefs, thoughts, and findings. Plow around your mind, sort the baggage, and unpack it. Commit to paper your moments. Watch your own personal drama unfold, and as days pass, even you will find your own story entertaining.

Why do readers like certain characters? Usually, the reason is that this person gets past obstacles to prevail. It's the basic Pixar formula that works every time out. Think how cool it is to see that you are not the only person on earth hurting, flailing, and screwing up. Even the bad guys in your writing are reminders of everything we don't want to be, with all those tragic flaws that Shakespeare thought his era owned. (He had no idea. Finding a moral position in today's wilderness is just as slippery a slope, if not more so.)

Decide what you are passionate about in life and write about that. You can plant it inside your protagonist or make it the cornerstone of your persuasive writing. Say what really matters to you, and contribute to the literature, as a citizen of the world who deeply cares about what happens.

Always reserve the right, though, to abandon your rational mind during writing stints. Humanize your characters into thinking, speaking people who have opinions and tendencies and eccentricities. Like an autopsy reveals, there is more to a cowboy wearing a Stetson than a smooth-talking, guitar-strumming renegade.

Trust that you have much to share and superb ways to do so. Let your ardent interest, your rah-rah spirit be unending. Allow your wildest mind-indulgence to flip and fly until it lands on a spot that feels right. Assume the stance that no one has to be Thomas Wolfe or Toni Morrison to have special insights into mankind and a desire to communicate them well. Your position on the earth matters as much as anyone else's.

Get a Few Do-Overs

Remember how valuable perseverance is in the writing game *and* the game of life. Think of stories you've read of writers who paper their bathrooms with rejection letters. Consider for a moment the advice I got years ago from a wise-cracking yet wise magazine editor-in-chief, who told me, "Just stick around long enough, and they will make you editor." She was right. They did. Five times I wound up editor-in-chief of different magazines. Early on, intuition told me to file away tips from older writers.

Let that tiny voice in your head—the one who is on your side—give you advice. You don't know this person by name, but she does live in the corridors of your brain. Maybe this is a lobbyist trying to get his way. Maybe this is a spiritual leader urging you to focus on dues-paying for that final-of-final days. But you need that hall monitor, so when she shuts down and you can't hear her anymore, walk away from the computer. Unwind. Take a walk, bake a cake, shop for jeans, or meet a friend for coffee. Get down off that perch with all the barbed wire and spikey things because it keeps visitors away by convincing you (and them) that nothing matters but writing.

See the beautiful people right in front of you. That perfect child of yours whom you adore. That precious husband who, for all his degrees and prominence, is just your sweet baby boy that you cover up at night because you hate knowing that he got cold sleeping in a chicken coop as a child.

People want your attention, and getting that from a writer is about like gliding up Niagara Falls, bottom to top. But you *can* be that rare writer who values people. Without them, you're nothing but a creaky raft drifting toward a glacier. Look around. Marvel at your good fortunes. Embrace them, one and all. Become known as "the hugger."

Choose Critique "Readers" with Care

And finally, for the love of God, *do not*, please,

tap your partner or spouse as a critique reader. Not if you want the relationship to survive. Think about it: If he or she reads your stuff, what exactly are the criticism options? This is really no different than the time you asked if a polka-dot skirt made you look big; "yes" and you hate him, "no" and you spot a lie. Is there a win here somewhere?

Readers can be brutal. They can be honest. They can be brutal *and* honest. Regardless, the person who fails to call your work "amazing" tumbles down your list of most loved. In fact, if you want unequivocal praise, just *hire* a reader. That's like hiring a fangirl or fanboy to applaud you; such people will tell you whatever you want to hear if they're getting paid.

And, when you're the one offering a critique, don't expect thanks for your astute observations. Quite the contrary. The person will be bitter and angry and probably never feel the same about you. Worse, that individual may fight back. It's like the old man whose wife takes away his car keys; he asks why, and she tells him in very diplomatic words that he's not the best driver on the road these days. He lashes out, "I'm better than you are!" And yada, yada, yada, the conversation goes downhill.

Understand this: no one LOVES criticism. People really just want to hear how wonderful the work is, end of story and exclamation mark. It reminds me of being in the sixth grade and seeing spiral-notebook "Opinion Books" passed around; we would read what others had to say about us ("Great smile! So sweet!). Nothing but positive comments hit those pages in the bubble-gum '60s, but kids still felt compelled to compare comments to see if the words were complimentary enough. If not, why not?

As you may have picked up on by now, locating someone whose opinion you value enough to critique your writing is tricky business; the person does not want the role—and fears your reaction to honest opinions. Your best bet is a mutual critique setup, which means locating a member of a writers' group or simply someone who writes, like you. Keep expectations low. If you hand a 555-page manuscript to this person, you can't expect to get it back in a week. People are busy, and your critique will never be tops in their priorities.

Best idea: agree on a timeline. For example, you give the person your work when he hands over his; plan to meet in a month to exchange whatever you two have managed to read. Do not make edicts or rules. If what you write is interesting, he'll gorge on it. If it's not, you're back to square one, anyway.

Write every day, but don't set target dates for *getting published*. Churn out a certain number of words or pages or chapters per week. Goals are good, but they can be destructive when you cling to them in earnest even when they work against you.

Writing will weasel its way into your mind and heart until you cannot let a day go by without tapping out some thoughts. Unlike golf, instead of giving you fits and fatigue, writing unravels the knots in you and hands you the gift of peace.

Topic Bounty

Endless topics intrigue. No matter what piece of literature a teacher assigns, you can do a glowing essay on it if you just believe in your words. Go to the word well (in your mind), gather up some treasures, and relish your incredible ability to write on boiled cabbage or funny-faced dolls, beehives, or bean sprouts.

If you ever decide to do freelance writing, the more topics you can handle, the better off you are. I've written on homicide, health, headaches, medicine, anxiety, panic attacks, fitness, celebrities, and even potty-training. Enlarging your scope takes practice, but a writer's mind will get it done. Pay checks are always good.

PART IV:
Give Personal Essays Pizzazz

Who doesn't love using "I" and "me" freely? And that's what can happen in your college essay, narrative, and memoir. To kick off Part IV, we zero in on the infamous college admissions essay that strikes fear in the souls of high school juniors and seniors when it actually *should* be party time, really. Because this is a narrative essay, you get to use "I" and "me" and "we" and even contractions. Go easy on casual, though. Don't get overly "slangy."

The second area covered in Part IV is the personal narrative or memoir, which often tells a story about an individual experience, situation, event, or life. For your project, you may want to try writing a short narrative based on your childhood. This prompt can inspire a narrative: *Describe a time in your life that you faced a critical decision, and the consequences that followed were far more earth-shaking than you expected.*

On the other hand, if you prefer, go your own way, and write that memoir or narrative essay you've been talking about for years. If you're dying to write your life story, dig in and investigate your childhood.

Chapter Twenty:
Personalize College Essays

Tip for the Day: Are you getting warmed up? Now that it's time to write college admissions essays, you're really good at essay writing. That means all you have do is put your own personality into the pieces you submit to colleges.

The college admissions essay doesn't matter all that much. You hear this all the time. However, when it's time to submit these essays, you will see friends and their parents huddling, intent on making theirs the best ones ever submitted. You wonder: All things being equal—rank in class, SAT and ACT scores, good grades, school activities, community service—what makes you stand out from hordes of qualified applicants? How can you prove you're one of the best choices?

Think about it. If you asked people who knew you or *knew of you* in high school, what would they say they found most memorable? He's the geeky guy who was always holding up political posters in the quad. She's the tall redhead who led the debate team. They are the off-the-wall free spirit singing solos at pep rallies. It goes on and on: the serious guy, the beach dude, the rowdy cheerleader, the funky dresser, the obnoxious team member, the super-smart speaker...

Once you break it down, the entire prospect of writing an essay is less frightening. In fact, it offers a wonderful opportunity to showcase your uniqueness. Tell the college admissions officers why you would be an asset to the University of California, Irvine, or University of Kentucky, or Rice University or Brown or Yale.

It is true that most college admissions counselors seek to consider a student holistically, from GPA to interviews to essays to volunteerism. So, the essay is just ONE aspect of the criteria that affects decisions. In a nutshell, write an essay that makes your best case for being a major contributor to that university's campus. Are you a talented leader? A voice for your generation? An exceptional musician? A class-act speaker? A champion athlete?

While lists of accomplishments and GPA give some insight into *you, the person*, admissions professionals want more. Ideally, they hope to learn something interesting about you that they cannot find among activities or academics or letters of recommendation.

What is your passion? While that may be the prompt for your college essay, there are many high school seniors who have not yet landed on one. They hope to find a passion in college. If you fall in that group, select a prompt that engages your interest but also is expandable enough to tweak the topic so that it encompasses your strengths. Those, you can list in a heartbeat.

Maybe you're an athlete. However, the most interesting part of your sports background is that you had to overcome injuries and surgeries to get to play basketball at all, much less stand out athletically. So, there's your best hook. Maybe you're the shyest girl in your senior class. However, by the time of graduation you had found a niche—Book Lovers' Club, for example—and you now express yourself loudly and clearly. So, there's your best hook.

Maybe you're the middle child in a family of two gigantic achievers. Or two children with autism. Or you're the child of a famous attorney or a world-class swimmer or an Emmy-winning actor. Hook. Hook. Hook. Maybe you had a seismic event during high school that shaped you more than anything else.

Whatever your topic, wind it along the path of how it reveals you. For example, as the middle child, you first learned to keep a low profile and then decided your best bet for getting attention was to post terrific grades. Or during senior year your family hosted an exchange student from Japan who changed your life; you became a better sharer, a networker of experiences, and had a "sibling" for the first time. You grew, and there's your hook for a great college essay.

General tips:

- Make the essay as creative and well-written as possible.
- Have someone proofread it for grammar and punctuation errors.
- Check to make sure it sounds formal enough—the opposite of a text message.
- Observe the required length. If the limit is 500 words, 250 is too short, and 502 is too long.
- Your goal: Give that influential admissions officer a reason to "fight" for your acceptance.
- Make your voice and your personality shine through.
- Make sure it's not ordinary.

College admissions counselors are trying to find

out several things:

- Can you write well?
- Are you going to be a contributor at the university?
- What are you like?

By the same token, it doesn't matter if you choose an oft-used topic, but it does hurt if you fail to give it a novel, fresh twist. You don't have to write about a special challenge or a "life burden" to have a winning essay. Yours can be incredible if you just focus on showcasing the most brilliant parts of you.

Choose a theme or go with a life-narrative. You don't have much space to communicate, and that makes it important to maximize each sentence of your message. You may want to find a favorite word or a favorite number to thread together the ideas you intend to convey.

Example: To understand who I am, you must understand how it feels to be one of 15 children in a family. (That blows anyone away; an admissions officer can't put this one down.)

Example: My life evolved, accidentally, in threes. I danced on three different teams. I went to three different schools. I considered three careers. However, today only one of these remains in contention, and that is the profession that crushed all others—medicine. Also, what I eventually learned from my numerology fixation is that you can't rely on lucky numbers. No one should go full-tilt lockstep into believing that if a development fails to fit the number code, it has to go. (This essay intro skips past the "boring" pile.)

Example: Do I want to be boots-on-the-ground or the leader-of-the-pack? Besides having a fondness for hyphenation, this is a quandary I often ponder. From getting way too much attention in elementary school, I began to value weird things, like kids calling me a "fashionista" just because I wore Uggs all the time. Anyway, what evolved was that my grandmother pushed me into running for "student gov," which I won every year as I marveled at the efficacy of a little democratic cosmos that does absolutely nothing but look cute. Thus, to say I was too much "in my head" during early school years would be an understatement. I was conducting an autopsy on every curriculum move my teachers made, and although I hid my scrutiny, a yawny malaise in my attitude told me it was a good thing that elementary school ended just as I morphed into rebel-without-a-cause. Then all my angst momentum grew in junior high, when I chose to attend an arts school even though I would barely get through the door before I decided that my artistic endeavors would have to be sideline activities; I was going for the dance-under-the-goalpost career of medicine, possibly E.R. physician.

Example: I am a jokester. What few people know about me, though, is how that connects to me academically, personally, and professionally. (This gets the reader's curiosity.)

Example: My grandfather liked succulents, and he often talked to me about them, took me in his greenhouse, and discussed their merits. What I took away from these frequent visits to flora-land was that I had a great deal in common with succulents: I am small, thus portable. I don't need much water to stay alive. I have a lasting quality; I remember what my fifth-grade teacher said about hasty generalizations and what my running coach said about maximizing locker space. Thus, like the succulent, I have staying power, and while I may not be the most gorgeous of the specimens, I inspire confidence merely because I am somewhat regal and quite enduring. (The off-the-wall quality of this essay introduction is good.)

Example: I decided to be a doctor because there wasn't any other career that I liked. For me, it was a process of elimination.

(What you *don't* want to say in a doctor essay is that you want to help people and you are very helpful and compassionate. Too clichéd.)

Example: My room is the roadmap to me.

Plastered with pictures of friends and pieces of art, the entire square footage resonates with the influences of my sixteen years. There are wafts of fragrance, myriads of color, and tear-stained pillows, and amid it all, I track papers from self-study so deep that it is the factor that helps me to emerge from my bedroom other-centered. Maturely, I can hold my grandmother's hand during Granddaddy's funeral. Confidently, I can reassure my website-collaborator of her excellent qualities that she takes for granted. Devil's advocate-ly, I can lift a friend from wallowing in a fantasy world of gaming.

In the multifaceted and textured roadmap that is my living space, I develop insights and a personal philosophy. Rather than basing these exclusively on religion, I take a whole-world Zen-ish approach that combines the Golden Rule ("Do unto others as you would have them do unto you") and top it off with a Thomas Edison wisdom that says, "If we did all the things we are capable of, we would literally astound ourselves." It's a lot, right? However, if someone absolutely forces me to choose the most pivotal element in the room, I would have to go straight over and pick up a framed photo of me in a Halloween costume with a Medusa headdress. Wound up in all those snakes going in different directions, I found my home; it was an amazing catharsis, the sensory aspect of realizing that for one thing, I would never surpass this costume for macabre points, and two, I clearly was overthinking everything in my entire life to the point of exhaustion. What kind of third-grader is plotting her entry into an arts high school? What kind of a high school freshman has a chart of colleges on her wall with detailed information on requirements, key dates, and student body ambiance? It is safe to say I am not lighthearted. However, with my madcap intensity also comes a quirky girl who laughs often and easily, whose go-to drink is chai tea, and who likes being a regular teen kid who loves Blake Shelton, and popcorn, and "Hamilton." A little ADHD goes a long way, right? I get it. Like I said, I got too much attention in elementary school. I blame it on the Uggs. (This essay definitely makes an admissions officer want to meet this charismatic candidate.)

The above are idea-starters. Read them, and they can keep you out of the mundane lane and steer you toward an extraordinary essay.

Real-World College Admissions Essays

The following are some sample college essays that helped a few seniors get numerous acceptance letters (we omit names and universities for privacy).

Prompt: Describe an example of your leadership experience in which you have positively influenced others, helped resolve disputes, or contributed to group efforts over time.

Essay: A difficult leadership experience allowed me to influence others positively. The story begins when an injury kept me off the volleyball court my senior year after I had played for three years. However, I was fortunate that my coach considered me a leader and asked me to be an assistant coach in order to keep me involved. In my new role, I challenged team members to play harder and smarter, managed practices, taught skills and strategy, and helped the coach make critical game decisions. It was a valuable experience because it provided numerous opportunities to increase my ability to communicate effectively and to hold people accountable.

One of the main lessons I learned was the difference between leader and friend. A leader must make decisions based on evidence, not emotion, in order to do what is best for the team. An example was when the coaches were allocating playing time. The head coach asked me to choose starters for a game, and thus I had to decide between a friend and another player. Along with the coaching staff, I encountered the harsh reality that it would be necessary to bench my friend during his senior year because he was not performing well. After that change was made, the team had better chemistry and won more often. The volleyball team benefited from this decision, which was a "mature" coaching move, having to choose the person who could contribute the most.

Sometimes, the right move from a supervisory point of view is uncomfortable, even when your gut instinct informs the decision. The end result may not be what you want, but at some point, you may decide that it is exactly what you need.

Prompt: What would you say is your greatest talent or skill? How have you developed and demonstrated that talent over time?

Essay: My greatest talent is instinctive sociability; I liaison successfully with all types of people. In elementary-school sports, I befriended everyone on my teams. Compassion and amiability allowed me to be friends with a sweeping majority of people who were my age. Of course, I am aware that this sociability comes as a lucky quirk of DNA *and* from the excellent role modeling of parents who exhibit generosity of spirit every day of their lives.

As I gained confidence, my adaptation to social situations developed proportionally. When I started at Mater Dei High School, my middle school friends

> **"**
> **Write an essay**
> **that makes your**
> **best case for being a**
> **major contributor to**
> **that university's**
> **campus.**
> **"**

were attending a different high school, and that meant I had to make new friends and maintain old relationships. To set the scene for this particular anecdote, I must mention that in Southern California, many young people envy Mater Dei students because the school has a reputation for turning out successful scholars. Thus, when I attended a religious retreat and the directors put me into a group of strangers (who knew each other), I realized that the retreat participants included both drug dealers and school dropouts. Then, I told my group that I attended Mater Dei and saw the school's stigma immediately cloud the atmosphere. The hostility was palpable.

In response, though, instead of being bitter, I became an *agent of change*. I campaigned to fix the Mater Dei stereotype, and by the end of the retreat, I had found common ground with everyone in my group and had introduced them to my Mater Dei friends. Before we all left to go home, one of my new buddies walked up and said, "I used to hate people who go to your school, but you changed my mind." That was my first realization that I had a natural talent for building bridges beyond stereotypes and befriending people from all walks of life. I have no doubt that this asset will help me navigate a positive college experience. Furthermore, this asset will help me change the world as a global citizen. *I know how to reach out, and in today's often confusing world, that is a plus indeed.*

Prompt: Beyond what has already been shared in your application, what do you believe makes you stand out as a strong candidate for admissions?

Essay: What makes me stand out as a candidate for admissions is perseverance. I obtained this valuable quality from my grandfather, Greg Munoz, who was one of my most important role models. By excellent example, he demonstrated how to work hard and excel. His parents came to America at the end of the Great Depression in pursuit of better lives for their children. One of eleven kids, my grandfather was determined to make a name for himself and refused to let poverty hold him back.

Certainly, he had humble beginnings. and, like me, he went to community college. He then graduated from UCLA and got his law degree at USC. Not only was he a hard worker, he was also an inspirational role model for his children and grandchildren alike. When the governor appointed him a Superior Court Judge in Orange County, many admirers applauded my grandfather's ability to overcome adversity. Of course, his children and grandchildren were watching, learning from his example.

During high school, I showed the influence he had on me when I set out to become a good athlete by spending countless hours in practice. Despite being injured over and over, I always came back with great spirit, and coaches recognized this tenacity as did my later work supervisors. I attribute my tenacity to the teachings that my grandfather instilled in me: no complaints, *only solutions*. Never give up. These are important life lessons that I will be forever grateful for having learned.

Prompt: What is the most significant challenge society faces today?

Essay: Some people say DNA is destiny, and this may be true, especially if a person has a talent that is hard-wired. However, for most people—the every-men, every-women of this world—what will get you ahead in life is the set of circumstances of your birth.

This question brings me to the challenge I want to address. As the world explodes with more people, more diseases, more poverty, more conflict, what trickles down is an increasing number of problems. Of these, inequality stands alone as the most significant challenge society faces. An overarching umbrella, equality encompasses disparity in income, opportunity, and financial status—inequities of an uneven playing field. While one person is wealthy, another is not—and the reasons are not always simple.

As a student of history, I have examined different segments of society in various cultures, and I am sure that the demographic into which a person is born does not have to be perpetuated but often is. Society can address inequality but making wishes into realities requires leaders with moral authority. Excuses, bromides, and clichés will not work.

Indeed, taking steps to tackle inequality by means of specific measures for change requires less talk, more action. Inequality should be distasteful to all of us, and adopting a zealot's intensity to improving society helps us face what is at stake and thus paves the way for improvements. To finesse demographic destiny, we must take the dare, do the deed.

Amassing contributions is what makes a cake a cake; uniting "gifts" is what makes a world a world. What is meaningful to me is the state of our world today and all the people who have contributed to making our country what it is. This includes leaders, citizens, scientists, activists, and administrators. I have benefited from the culmination of the wisdoms of many people, whose works amount to thousands of years of human effort. In effect, though, the one thing that never changes is the way the world tracks on tremendous human resources of minds, hearts, energies, and time.

The more I know about the world, the more I will be able understand its unlimited possibilities and adapt my philosophies so that I can be a force for good in the microcosm in which I live. That is why we learn, why we even bother to rise above the tiny teacup of what we knew at age one. Growth equals enlightenment equals progress. The shapeshifter inside makes me ever eager to embrace new knowledge, listen to opinions, and emerge a better global citizen.

The Essay's Hook

Most importantly, for your college admissions essay, write a strong hook that gets a reader's attention. The following is a good example: "Two years ago in my biology class, I became engrossed with our study of the human brain. Hot, right? Maybe not everyone would see it that way, but I have to say that I instantly fell in love with neurotransmitters, the cerebellum, and even the frontal lobe until I could not stop thinking about these things, and soon it became a fulltime obsession. I began to think, *yes, I could be a brain surgeon.* After all, I was crazy about the TV series "Grey's Anatomy." Thus, my thought processes circled the wagons of my own brain, listing career options from the ridiculous to the sublime, until I realized that choosing a profession was as much a process of elimination as one of selection.

You can be outspoken or outrageous or understated. Ask yourself what you would like for an admissions officer to know about you and write that. Pepper it with excellent vocabulary and writing flair. Dance like there is no one watching—on paper.

Chapter Twenty-One:
Polish Your Narratives

Tip for the Day: Make writing your new best friend. You'll find worlds of joyful self-expression in narratives and memoirs. Travel memory lane and start writing your "life story."

We include the following excerpts from memoirs to give you a sense of content that drives narrative essays and memoirs. To write your own, go back to your earliest memories, both light and dark, and record impressions. What you end up with in the form of a narrative essay or memoir may surprise you. (Don't be afraid to indulge your voice and even embroider on what actually happened if you want to experiment with a "fictionalized" version.) Write without fear that the thought police will show up at your door. Indulge your wildest thoughts and dreams.

Writer, Writer, Catch on Fire
By Diane Stafford

How compelling, the lure of the *dark side*…and the appeal of writers Stephen King, Truman Capote, and Edgar Allan Poe, who pen horror tales that thrill the strange people who thrive on spooky vibes. Personally, I always loved "Creature from the Black Lagoon" and haunted houses; then, in recent years, I fixated on eerie series such as *Ozark, You,* and *The Following.*

But the real jackpot of cold chills came when I sat eye to eye with evil. A Texas Ranger arranged for me to interview serial killer Henry Lee Lucas in Georgetown, Texas, where he awaited his trip to Death Row in Huntsville. I was all in, of course, thinking that no one personified evil better than the man behind numerous murders.

I *wanted* to hear this man's story. In fact, I was almost levitating until I told my parents, and my dad chided me for "glorifying a killer." That slowed me down, and then the ethics of the project became a moot point when Lucas confused his messaging and swore that he also orchestrated the Jim Jones' Kool-Aid suicides, Princess Diana's death, and even the University of Texas Tower killings. He had enjoyed the lively jailhouse days of quasi-celebrity and milk shakes so much that he decided to take credit for some *famous* homicides to extend his days in the sun.

Oblivious to his misstep, Lucas merely glared at visitors with his good eye (the other was glass) and jabbered on and on about "the fun of having reporters around...." A strange specimen of vermin for sure, but after he lost all credibility, and the American public rejected him, the book project plummeted, and I was left with audio tapes, photos, and yellow legal pads full of notes.

Getting My Latte On

Like anyone looking for a new idea, I went to Starbucks. Driving to the one nearest my home in Newport Beach, California, I was craving my prized beverage when I met a bright-eyed elite runner/barista who, many lattes later, would become my co-author for this book. (That's a story in itself because over the three-year span of writing, Melissa divorced, moved to two different states, and fell in love.)

At any rate, she and I quickly came up with a spiffy (*not grisly*) book concept the first time we met at a Coffee Bean, of all places. Then, as books tend to go, our idea shifted in several directions. A year ago, deciding to slant it as a post-COVID guide for motivating young writers, we buckled down and wrote our way to the finish line. (We changed the title 11 times and edited until we wore the letters off our computer keys.)

Eventually, as writing often goes, *this book is what it is.* Keeping that odd comment in mind, I must disclose right here, up front, a pet peeve that my husband and I used to laugh about because we shared the same one: the dreaded cliché.

Please don't say:

- At the end of the day
- Whatever
- That said
- No problem (especially if you're a Starbucks employee)

Nothing is worse than being in the drive-through ordering an invigorating drink than to thank the barista and then hear Krista or Crash say, "No problem." Of course, it's not a problem—it's your job. What happened to "thank you"? I hate it when an old favorite like that disappears from the landscape. Thank-you was so portable, so exactly what our parents taught us…

Social Media Yikes

On the upside, though, those Starbucks kids are incredibly sweet, smiley, and well trained, and I'm pretty sure they would be the last ones to lash out on social media. Or at least that's the image I have of them, and I prefer to keep it.

That brings up a major pet peeve that actually *matters*. The hatefulness that social media spews day and night gets my vote as the darkest force affecting our society today. The thundering question is: *Why do people think we need to hear every thought that flips through their minds?* Facebook and Twitter hatch malice and arrogance simply because these handy platforms require zero qualifications. The jarring truth is, some people cannot resist filling strangers' ears with every misery of their daily lives (not to mention embellished vacations, clothes, and families). The louder the mouth, the bigger the clout.

Here's the irony, though. Sharing your scummiest self is the opposite of what will make you happy. Ask Mother Teresa. Ask Gandhi. Ask any person you admire, and you will learn that nothing has made their lives richer than showing up for someone else. Giving. *This is the secret to happiness.* It is much like good parenting: all those days you provide unconditional love and get, in return, just eyerolls, sarcastic comments, and sleepless nights are

319

reminders that giving matters *even when it is not attached to instant gratification.*

In fact, one of the first things you learn from teaching, or parenting, or volunteer work, is that "getting outside yourself" makes you better than you were before. Who cares if your six-year-old gags on the new casserole that took you two hours to make? Who cares if your fifteen-year-old can't find it in her heart to help with chores no matter how many times you ask? Who cares if your spouse is angry because you forgot the sprig of mint in his tea even though this is the same person who can't remember your sister's name after 12 years of marriage?

We all started out demanding creatures until someone told us along the way that we were supposed to shed this feral condition as we grew older. It isn't hard. Just remind a child how wonderful he or she is—and you will see more and more of that very self. Good behaviors bloom when watered by encouragement and praise. Criticism and nagging fail because the recipients are always looking for the exit door.

Who Is the Fairest Sibling of Us All?

In childhood, one of the funniest detours that people take is comparison shopping. A sibling is getting more attention, inspiring the itchy question "hey, was I adopted?" Or at school, the showoff kid is a neon magnet while you get less attention than green chalk. (Or someone just has better clothes or cooler shoes.)

Sitting on the sideline, you wonder why your specialness is being missed by so many people. Then, years later, you read online that someone thinks you have a "dumb laugh" or a "freaky smile" or a "weird personality." Instead of considering the source, you absorb the critique and become just another social-media-bruised person shuffling down the highway of life. It happens a thousand times a day.

On the other hand, by writing your own narrative essay, you can recapture the YOU of childhood—that adorable, audacious, fearless kid with an angelic aura. Find a picture of you at six, maybe seven, and give a shoutout to the kid-with-promise that you once were. Embrace the stunning parts that you left behind growing up, on your way to becoming a list-making, conflict-mongering, sad-sack-whining adult.

- Stick that childhood photo in a spot by your computer as a reminder to operate out of a happier mind space.
- Vow to do something incredible. Despite being stuck in today's glittery achieving lane, U-turn and grab that old-time sweetness in you.

- Start with a pen or pencil or computer and write. Capture memories of playing with friends in the yard on warm nights of summer. The winking, blinking forces of nature are still out there, just a bit harder to see when you're an adult. You have to look, though. Remember things you loved to do as an unstoppable child, and revisit them one more time.

Were You Funny, Solemn, Scrappy?

Much of what we are is inborn, parent-nurtured, or good luck. Everyone knows someone whose phenomenal success in business or relationships is jaw-dropping mainly because it doesn't add up; the person is not especially bright or attractive or the nicest human on the block. The peak of his education was reading *Call of the Wild* in junior high. No matter. We still see that person arrive at the 20-year high school reunion via stretch limo, with gorgeous spouse and clothes that make his penchant for retail therapy craven fact. All around the school gym, amid crepe-paper decorations, people wonder how this happened, with the second thought being, "So, where did *I* go wrong?"

Part DNA, part luck, part family—yes, a patchwork quilt of influences makes you the person you are today. Maybe your childhood path was bumpy, and the adult superhighway still is. Now, at age "whatever," you continue to search for a niche. And guess what? You *should* do that because being The Only You in All the World makes you designed for a specific slot. Self-interest doesn't make you narcissistic.

First, though, stop worrying about people rating you. What separates those who love their lives *from those who don't* boils down to accepting the person you are. Don't get stuck in the rut of perpetual envy and payback. If you know a person like that (or if, God forbid, it's you), please understand that a faultfinder mechanism comes from a place of massive insecurity. Unable to accept your own imperfections, you point out others' flaws. Make them smaller and you get bigger, maybe?

Anyway, chip away at those niggly parts, and you'll be happier in no time. Criticize others, and you are simply a harsh critic, for what that's worth (*not much*). Take off that long black judge-y robe and get out some cheerleader pompoms and pull for your partner, your children, your friends. Every person needs supporters, and you can be one.

Your Reboot

Take 15 minutes a day to write about your childhood—grade by grade, year by year. Explore what worked and what didn't. Recall little stories, exciting successes, special people, disappointing outcomes—all of it. Start with something like, "The year I was ten, I realized somebody needed to be in charge of my family, or nothing was ever going to get done." Then let your mind fill in what comes next—a hurdle or a funny anecdote or sibling rivalry run amok. Free your imagination, and look for a place where you can write without interruption.

Truly, the silliest thing about adults is that we grow stubborn, reluctant to autopsy a wrong fork in the road, even something as life-changing as a past marriage. Most of us avoid real reflection because, frankly, it is upsetting. Avoidance, though, dooms us to repeat mistakes. Yes, there were times when you could have been kinder; acknowledge this and learn from it.

You can do better. Listen more. Talk less. Center yourself (*I get to say that because I live in California*). Think of turning points, and there you have meat for your story sections, such as "My Writing Outclassed Everybody in Class" or "What I Learned from Not Making the Basketball Team" or "I Was Always the Boy Carrying a Book." (These, by the way, came from

324

teens.) Each of these topics can inspire paragraphs that you develop with your own fresh and funny and frank observations.

Some good pieces of advice I've heard are these:

- If several people offer the same observation on your habits, *listen up,* and think about what they said.

- If you fall in love, ask your partner this screening question: *Is there someone in your past that you couldn't refuse if that person asked for a do-over?*

- Remember that being a loving partner is more important than being right in arguments.

- If your relationship makes you cry, leave it. And, stop being a partner who makes people sad.

- Encourage your children to be themselves. Every chance you get, shower praise on them for being the originals they are.

- Say the word "no" to children as seldom as possible. Instead, fill them with positives about the promising little people they are.

- Try to go a full day without setting the record straight. Let other people have opinions un-stomped-on by you.

- Jot down key moments in your past. Are you

interested in taking another look at some of
the people and professions you left behind
when you decided they weren't smart choices?
Why not check out the options you discarded?

- Ponder the strengths your parents saw in you.
- Show the adoration you feel. (Every day when
  I got home from school, my mother gave me
  a smile that melted all fears. I knew I could
  run in the door carrying a rat in my mouth
  and she would still love me.)

Developing a Point of View

Few people understand writers. If I had ever
been on "The Bachelorette," they would have accused
me of being "too much in my head." That is where I
live. I rarely listen to advice because I have committee
members in my head, who do my long-range planning
of about twenty minutes.

When I was a child, my point-of-view agitated
me so much that I couldn't sit still. My older sister
slapped my "jimmy legs." My parents said "settle
down" until they lost their voices.

Eventually, I became such a drawback to take to
church that my parents quit re-standing me up (I
squirmed and slipped under the pews). They had to
endure the stares of people around us as I requested
scraps of paper from my mother's purse and sang in a

low (weird) alto voice.

Bromance

Then came the ever-popular sibling push-pull for dominance. As youngest, my brother Allen—a five-year-old gunslinger with western shirt, chaps, spurs, and plastic guns—got away with murder because the white-blond curls and water-color blue eyes were just too much. Keenly aware of hierarchies, I did not fail to notice when he slyly stole some of my fanfare. But God knows he *was* darling—and I, eight years older, was too old for dolls, darn it, so I babied him and adopted an Alice in Wonderland look: waist-length blonde hair, pink ribbons, and a little boy in my sidecar. Allen's tiny hand tucked in my own, I led him around like a little pony.

Of course, he sometimes overplayed the cuteness card. In particular, I remember bracing for major blowback when we visited our Aunt Bonnie and Uncle Moody in Lafayette, Louisiana, where my aunt gasped at the sight of Allen while nearly knocking down my sister and me to hug him first. "Oh, my goodness, there's Clinton Allen!" she would say, lilting southern-belle saccharin. She had two daughters, no sons, which was enough to make my brother her drug of choice.

Unfailingly, though, Allen's impish smile always

made me patient with rascally behavior, which would forever be my Achilles's heel. Besides being the ultimate diplomat, he was a talented builder by age nine, when he created a full-fledged, three-room treehouse out of ten twigs, sixteen branches, and Elmer's glue. Preschooler Allen Shirley was the most adorable small-fry fort-constructor in Texas at the time. In fact, he is still a magician of building, and I've never stopped marveling. My mind was blown just trying to piece together my daughter's Barbie-mobiles for Christmas. More than two parts, and I was begging for help.

Despite our difference in ages, Allen and I maintained sibling solidarity. When he was a teen, I bought him his first record, "Hair," from the musical, and persuaded Mother and Daddy that his hippie mane was harmless. Our success in that joint venture inspired him to pass on the absolution; as president of his senior class, Allen Shirley championed his classmate bros, who were getting expelled from school for having long hair. He boldly went to the principal's office and secured safe passage from detention-land for all the long-hair dudes, and, while he was at it, also saved the girls in trouble for too-short skirts.

Sister Act

As for our older sister, she never got in the way of anyone because Camilla was barely a resident of our house, this ghostly teenager slipping in and out on waves of wispy quiet to evade parental scrutiny. She was way smart and *almost* Elizabeth Taylor, as well as being in love and completely above the fray. Other than warning that "familiarity breeds contempt" and barring her from seeing her true love more than once a week, my father had his hands full, curbing his two younger, wildcat urchins. Why look for problems with

> **"**
> **Watch out what you wish for unless you're willing to bet on the Door of Unknowns over the Door of Knowns.**
> **"**

his bookish oldest?

Camilla had a certain charm about her, and even today, when I call, she answers, always, with a jolly "Is this my *baby sister*?" Melts my heart as I open up to all the softness of childhood, tumbling back into place, which makes me thank God, that very moment, for my insanely safe and happy "family of origin."

I have always admired my sister's talent as a painter and wished I understood how those beautiful pictures came into being. She was the quiet one whose albatross was a core belief that having an old-fashioned name had held her back. No one could pronounce "Camilla," so they either refrained from saying her name or called her "Camelia" or "Camille." I saw how dramatically a name can affect a kid's life, which inspired me to focus fully when I worked on writing my baby-name books. I knew that names mattered.

Most couples struggle to come up with three names they like for their babies-to-be, and most kids prefer a "safe" name. If you give your baby an unusual name, just make sure it's easy to say and remember. Homemade concoctions are tough to pronounce and even harder to spell and often end up being a nuisance from cradle to bingo-days.

Take Me to Church

For me, church was about music. To this day, I love-love-love the hymns we sang in the Baptist Church, and I still remember the words to them—*Old Rugged Cross, In the Garden, Amazing Grace*—and the best of all, *O Holy Night*. Even now, I break into song and pretend that I can carry a tune. In high school choir, I was a "smiler" so that tells you something; our choir director didn't worry about damaging fragile child egos because scoring well in district choir competition was the point of having a choir. Voice discrimination was no one's concern. (Besides, we all knew Wanda Brandt was the one who could sing.)

Anyway, let me be clear: I gave religion a chance. The problem was, early in life, I saw inconsistencies in organized religion. At first, I went along with things, mainly because the preachers spoke in tough, loud terms, and I had never heard yelling at home—thus, these really angry men captivated me. I grew up Southern Baptist, and we attended services on Sunday mornings, and in my family, attendance was mandatory. For the kid with a conjured-up illness, failure to attend church on Sunday morning meant censure of fun activities the rest of the day. Thus, the dreary boredom of the church would rule all waking Sunday hours instead of just one.

So, I went. Whining. Complaining. Wiggling.

331

Bigger problem, I developed doubts about religion. In weekly sermons, our preacher yelled about hellfire and brimstone and cleansing ourselves of the stain of sin. I would sit there thinking, "How bad can a ten-year-old be?" It sounded like dopiness to me, but no rebellious backtalk was allowed so I couldn't put a name on it.

The teachings were confusing, too. For example, we were taught that people who were Church of Christ were hell-bound because they believed they were the only ones going to heaven. And in the Baptist Church, all you had to do was be saved by "professing your acceptance of Jesus Christ." Then you could go about your regular business of being naughty and bratty. That was efficient and flexible. So, one Sunday morning when a revivalist pastor was summoning sinners to move down the aisle to the front of the church and "accept their savior," I popped up off the pew and joined the wave of misty-eyed people walking like zombies.

The same week, I was baptized—our preacher dunked me under water, and that was that. My parents were unduly proud of my act, which confused me. I was a decent kid before being immersed—why would I be different afterward? When I asked Mother, she sighed and ruffled my hair. "Some things, you have to just take on faith," she said, wondering

(I'm sure) why she had given birth to a kid who never stopped asking questions.

Really, being baptized didn't make me better, but I was apparently quite cleansed of sin. So, there's that. Besides, I've always liked the merits of a do-over. Still, when I continued to express doubts about the Bible's edicts, Mother began raising her right eyebrow in a big show of her roughest discipline—and I would shut up.

"So, what's going to happen to Uncle Brando, who left his wife?" I asked her one day. The 'D' word (divorce) was never, ever spoken in the Shirley family, and when I came across a photo of Uncle Brando kissing his wife, my dad took it away from me. Sex and love were taboos. For that reason, when I was twelve, and boys with googly-puppy-dog eyes started coming by the house to see me after school, I knew my parents began counting the days till I would leave for college.

Firefly Preservation

By teen years, I had a philosophy halfway pinned down. Early in childhood I had learned a lesson from being outdoors with friends, dancing around on lawns. Many nights I caught fireflies in a fruit jar, put the top on, and let them flash and flicker until I let them go. It was a close call for those "lightning bugs," as we called them. Frankly, with my love for things sinister, it could have gone either way.

I did become skeptical of Mother's adages that she sprinkled around to curb her kids' quirks. *Most of things we worry about never happen. Things always turn out for the best. Everything happens for a reason.* Well, no. I'd seen floods, and I'd seen hurricanes. I knew for sure that life was nuttily unpredictable, but I didn't annoy Mother with opinions that would make her raise that authoritarian eyebrow. She was too perfect for me to tinker with. In fact, she was such a goddess role model that I credit her with keeping me halfway normal. The thought of disappointing her was just too horrific. I was random, all right, but she had carved me a code of ethics I had to *try* to follow.

To be fair for historical accuracy, though, I was indeed The Activist, always agitating and petitioning my parents for more things to do. Nothing slowed me down. I savored every aspect of living and even mastered the family dynamic by tamping down my exuberance to act more like a Miss America contestant and less like a mental-health poster girl. Writing poems sedated my buzzing mind, most of the time. Though my ultra-Baptist Daddy warned me that I was "skating on thin ice" for every act of civil disobedience, I made my mother's eyes sparkle like tiny Disney lights when I wrote over-the-top love sonnets, idolizing her on paper.

Daddy would get no poems from me until he let up on the rigid discipline, and that never happened. I was mouthy enough to get in trouble by sundown every day, but it wasn't important because I was born to shine at school. I was on a roll of some kind that I had no understanding of at all, but the basics of it were:

- Write as much as possible.
- Write what I knew.
- Write until I got really good at it.
- Befriend everyone and be a leader.
- Smile all the live-long day.

Where the Boys Were

Yes, I was a lively, friendly girl. That meant that by the time I blew out thirteen candles on my cake, I was officially boy crazy. My parents escaped into Hear No Evil, See No Evil, Speak No Evil and pretended I wasn't there. Daddy no longer let me slather his cheeks in kisses, and it was clear that I had been demoted, leaving my brother at the top of the heap as an unflinching, worm-skewering "fishing buddy." I was left in no-man's-land, with nothing except my grades, and I had been making straight-As for so long that no one cared. My dad would peer at my report card and say, "That's what I expected." How desperately I wanted to hear "good girl," but I never got it.

Of course, in truth, I was never *alone* because I had friends, male and female, who were wholesome, fun, and funny, so much so that when teen years come to mind today, I really recall no angst at all. I do, however, prefer to spin my childhood as *somewhat thorny* simply because all stories, even memoirs, need *conflict, conflict, conflict,* and I like to deliver that. The reality is that in the '60s and '70s, homes and schools in Pasadena, Texas, were closer to "Father Knows Best" than "Grease" or "Urban Cowboy."

They Had My Back

After giving up on curing my restlessness, my parents turned to correcting my flawed posture. "*Straighten up*" was their new command. As I saw my loving parents morph into Back Police, I tried to avoid them. Still, life rocked along, with slumpy posture a central theme in our house on Butler Drive in Pasadena, Texas, and I was sneaking out the door every chance I got, the 'Where's Waldo' of our household.

However! If my wonky posture was purposeful (as they believed), and I'm not saying it was, it is important to mention that I grew up in an era of short girls, like my idol Annette Funicello. My friends were short. So, being a towering five-foot-six made me the Jolly Green Giant. Basically, I thought my discomfort would wane a bit if I lurched around like a kumquat-on-wheels and wrote funny little poems about odd shoulders.

Mother signed me up for dance classes to fix my "weak" shoulder muscles. I was always up for a fun time, and thankfully, it worked. Plus, I was deliriously happy dancing the calypso in a sarong, highland fling in kilts, "Sugarplum Fairy" in a tutu. For my part, I found costumes, toe dancing, and tap steps exhilarating; I wasn't even good at dance, but I could make lots of noise, tapping my way down our driveway in a snug satin outfit and black-patent leather dance shoes. I had my best friend Joan Jorden dancing right beside me. The stars were aligned. What more could a kid want?

Effervescence got attention. Peers elected me vice-president of the student body, Who's Who, editor of *The Beacon*, and Junior Achievement Sweetheart. Next, I was off to Sam Houston University, where I won "Best Pledge" of Alpha Delta Pi (because I cried when a member yelled at me), and four fraternities named me sweetheart. Despite my obvious penchant for social butterflying, I graduated summa cum laude.

I really, truly loved people. Eventually, though, it hit me that some folks shunned others for no reason. Discovering the duplicity of a few made me distrustful of many, and as I matured, that short-circuited my ebullience, although I didn't let the downgrade touch my writing. There I could conjure up any world I wanted, including one free of cruelty. I knew how to crawl into that cozy cubby and let thoughts seep onto paper while I luxuriated in the ecstasy of writing's warmth and freedom.

By college, my religion was really flagging. How could you trust church leaders? Reading the newspaper, I saw that many clergymen had episodes of nastiness—and if that was what came of the "calling of God" profession, what hope was there for the rest of us? Before I even learned the word "hypocrisy," I knew this stuff reeked. The very men yelling at us in church about dark-hearted sinners were apparently talking to themselves.

The one significant takeaway was *Do unto others as you would have them do unto you.* Wasn't that the gist of the whole religious thing, anyway? Surely if I could just follow that, I could skip church and wind up with an extra hour to write on Sunday mornings.

Best Summer Job Ever

At age nineteen, I accidentally hit the big time. My father read about a state "test" to find two Texas girls for NASA jobs. He encouraged me to take the selection test because the winners would be rewarded with summer jobs following freshman and sophomore college years. Then, a week after the exam, NASA's HR director called to tell me I had won a job in the Astronaut Office, with astronauts Neil Armstrong, Alan Shepard, Jim McDivitt, Dave Scott, Gus Grissom, Ed White, Roger Chaffee, etc. In the close-knit office at NASA in Clear Lake City, Tessa Slager (the other high scorer) and I assembled speeches for astronauts. Everyone called us "secretaries" because no one could imagine girls handling anything as weighty as speech writing for American heroes.

Writing as Comfort Food

I journaled as a kid, wrote nightly in a diary—and I wrote short-short stories. I kept only the one I submitted for a creative writing class as an eighteen-year-old college freshman. The professor, Leon Hale, was an award-winning columnist for the *Houston Chronicle*, and I still have the treasured note he paperclipped to my story. While I've misplaced love letters and trophies, hamsters and horses, I have managed to hold onto my special note.

Here's what he wrote to me:

Miss S—Now then, if you want to, we can sell this story. It's just first class. The plot is old as Jerusalem, but that doesn't hurt a bit because you've got it in the freshest wrapping on the market. And in this case, I'd start at the top—send it off to Redbook *or* Cosmopolitan, *and write a letter saying that you had the experience of working as a secretary to the astronauts, and know whereof you speak. Think it's important to tell 'em that. A couple of things I'd like to discuss with you about the story. So, stop by after class, even if you don't want to sell it. Listen, I don't know if I ever made this clear to you, but you have a tremendous talent for creative writing, and if you don't do something with it, you're doing yourself an awful injustice. I've been reading stories in this course for three years now, and with the possible exception of one person, you're the only student I've had that I thought could sit down and write a short story that a big magazine would buy. If I'd had, at your age, the talent and maturity of thought that you have now, why, I'd already be a millionaire. —Leon Hale.*

Leon Hale liked my writing! I bring this up mainly to emphasize the difference that educators make in students' lives. For me, it was a sign that I was *not* nuts to think I could be a writer. Someone saw *something* in me.

First Gigs

Fresh out of college, I had heavenly days teaching high school English and sponsoring the yearbook and newspaper. By age 30, my articles had been published in national magazines, and I'd landed my first New York agent. However, I truly grew up when my agent submitted three chapters of a proposed nonfiction book on the serial killer I had interviewed, and I accidentally received the rejection letter that had been meant for my agent's eyes only. A publishing-house editor had written: "Great writing style, and the story is strong. I would snap it up, but I'll never publish a writer from Texas. So, it's a no." I held that letter and stumbled into my bedroom and read it a second time, then a third. Tears trickled down my cheeks. Even before that, people had told me to move to New York or nothing would ever happen for me in publishing. That made me wonder exactly how much I wanted success.

Shattered, I realized I needed a thicker shell even though I was already half-turtle. I could shrink back and stay that way for hours at a time. Now, with my new knowledge of book politics, it turned into days and weeks. I crawled deeper inside myself. That lightbulb moment had taught me that bias did indeed exist, and adults just had to adjust to a world of hatemongering. I realized that prejudice was inescapable, no matter how hard people tried to force-feed change. Unless you were famous surgeon Michael DeBakey, you didn't get to go inside hearts and make repairs. Those who believed in equality would just have to model it and hope for the best.

The Bylines

While teaching journalism and English at South Houston High School in South Houston, Texas, I submitted stories to magazines. My first freelance check was $200 for a short story on a car that I sold to a magazine called *Corvette Fever*. I loved that byline unlike any I'd had before. Eventually, I had hundreds of articles and features published, fourteen books, and I edited reams of other people's writing. I interviewed everyone from Olympic gold-medal skater Tara Lipinsky and boxing champ Evander Holyfield to epitome-of-evil Henry Lee Lucas, before they bussed him away to Death Row.

Interestingly, though, my friends only wanted to hear about Lucas. What was he like? What did he say? Were you scared when alone with him? (More to come on this topic in my memoir! Leave your email address on dianestafford.org, and I'll let you know when the memoir is available for preorder.)

The Agent Way

I wrote for many magazines until 1985, when a partner and I founded one called *Houston Health & Fitness*. It was a natural offshoot of the leg warmer/aerobics days, when Houstonians got high on staying fit, taking supplements, getting massages, and applying electrodes to muscles. Everyone was doing it, and the timing for *H&FM* was spot-on.

For staffers, this was glam work—fitness and health stories and photos that were brought to readers courtesy of the sales success of gorgeous women selling advertising that made the magazine a stellar earner. Renee Redden and Sharon St. Romain were the superstars—charming sales executives whom no one could refuse, and things went our way in a swift success story. Truthfully, I couldn't begin to list all of those who made *H&FM* a success because the contributors were endless, from Cindi Rose and Carolyn Farb (on the socialite end of things) to Lee Labrada on the Mr. Universe muscleman side, to plastic surgeon Dr. Russell Kridel, rejuvenator of faces, famous and otherwise.

I wrote and edited and networked. My business partner David Nordin directed sales. People fell in love with *Health & Fitness Magazine* because it was easy to imagine themselves on the cover, which often happened. It was a homespun fun publication.

During the *H&FM* years, I continued freelance writing. My first agent died, so I sent out letters seeking a new agent, and I landed Elizabeth and Ed Knappman of New England Publishing, a terrific pair who brought me book contracts for years.

Ed persuaded me to tackle a book called *60,001 Best Baby Names*. Luckily, it became a bestseller, and royalty checks soon convinced me that writing books was easier than running a magazine, which led me to sell *Health & Fitness Magazine* and focus on books. Once I had fourteen in print, I dug in to edit and write more books.

The Year of Names made me a compulsive reader of movie credits. I couldn't turn off my personal search engine, always seeking new names, more names, made-up names, and bizarre names. As I look back, I see that my ADHD was so overpowering I did well to tack on just one other companion addiction. Gambling electrified me until COVID barred casino doors in 2020, instantly curing me of jackpot-adrenaline-seeking.

Eyes Askance

Even writers don't understand writers. A friend will find you quaint in a knickknack kind of way. The offspring of creatives are smart enough not to see this as a competition and fare the best. My child, instead of hating my obsession because it made her feel left out, saw it as a blessing because "only children" normally get helicopter-parented into a shrink's chair, but not my girl.

To this day, I marvel at my stunning, sweet daughter (now a physician) and think, "I could never get enough of being with her in a million years." We are incredibly close, and Jennifer is a happy person and a wonderful doctor. She knows me better than anyone does and has always sensed that a person with words rushing on a reel through the brain is as different from a non-writer as a giraffe is unlike a grasshopper.

On Marriage

The ideal spouse for a writer? Someone who does not rely on a partner for accounting. In particular, if you're a female writer, *you* should search for a man with a full-fledged life of his own, into which writer-girl can dash and slither in serpentine moves. Frankly, I could be designated learning-challenged when one considers how long it took for me to understand the rhythms of marriage and husbandly expectations.

In 2004, I relocated from Houston, Texas, to Newport Beach, California, because my daughter and her husband were moving here with my two-year-old grandboy-obsession. That was how I found my online-dating dream.

Greg Munoz accepted my orchestra of eccentricities, a maestro who understood the blonde gal tapping out sounds on a triangle while trying to sample everything from the bassoon to the ukulele. Anytime he got bored with my overamped writing antics, he would sort fishing lures, collections, and the garage that his friends called "The Hardware Store."

Still, I advise people, as a general rule, *do not marry a writer*. Otherwise, you—ordinarily a non-yeller—will end up perturbed when you realize your newfound love is incapable of answering a phone or using a broom, just two of many Pavlov responses that do not live in the brains of writers. Quirky people can be frustrating, no matter how much you like them, but I wed the most patient human being on earth.

Changes in Latitude

When I married Greg, I became the stepmother of five young adults overnight. I was so instantly smitten with them that everyone thought our Brady Bunch had to be The Big Lie or too cray-cray to take seriously. The truth was, these relationships just clicked, and my husband was happily amazed. All five bright and sweet kids inherited great traits from both parents; my sizzling-smart Greg and their personality-

346

plus mom, Melinda (daughter of film icon John Wayne) were superb parents, and she and I became close friends. (To be sure, a current wife and an ex-wife are an odd couple, and just to make people squirm even more, Melinda calls me her "sister-wife" around strangers, whose jaws drop.)

Anyway, I give credit for a madly happy family to our 18 grandkids, so astonishingly perfect in every way, *just like your children and grandchildren are, I'm sure.* I don't want to sound like a total Pollyanna, but they keep me excited about waking up; I am thankful for the abundant sunny days, sunny smiles, sunny lives.

Back in the Word Saddle

Always and ever, I returned to the MacBook Pro: my books/papers zone, a sweet home. That's why I love author Stephen King's comment that writing is "one of the few things where I do it less now and get as much out of it. Usually with dope and booze, you do it more and get less out of it as time goes by" (Greene).

I can relate. Writing is a wild passion and a comforter, an angora shawl around my shoulders and a hug at day's end—or beginning. When not writing regularly, I talk too much, and I hyper-focus on teaching children until they look worried when they see me coming. The buzzsaw brain of a writer won't stop because it is always on its way somewhere.

Those Readers of Yours

If you're a writer who wants to get published, don't expect much feedback from those who read your writing (for criticism). In fact, I really don't advise it unless you're a fan of frowns and yawns. These folks are called, in the biz, "readers," but a better term would be "scanners."

One thing is clear. *No one takes writers seriously.* People don't get what we're doing or that some of us support ourselves and our children that way. It is a job, after all. But no one believes it is because writing resembles too closely the leisure pursuits of journaling or daydreaming. Super easy to be dismissive about this profession, as in, "So you're still doing that little magazine?" Or: "Did you ever finish that little story of yours?"

It's like asking if I'm still a vegan or if I have moved on to hot chicken wings or if I still have bangs. Most people think that writing lacks gravitas. No one gets where your short story came from, but the assumption is that your creativity outpost has to be a fairly spooky place, and the less they know about it, the better.

What a writer *does* have in excess is loneliness that engenders idiosyncrasies. Far too many famous writers become alcoholics due to extended periods of isolation and quirky gene pools. Therefore, you can imagine the fates of writers who make a living writing, not that we care much about outcomes because we are so constantly buggered by self-doubt, self-recrimination, and self-flagellation. And those are the good days.

Amazing, really, that some writers are halfway normal, with good childhoods as launching pads. I had that advantage, and I also realized as years went by that, wait a minute—hey, maybe, just maybe, *I* was the family disruptor. Being way too good to myself, I had attributed the black sheep role to either my brother, who went through that unfortunate "oops" year of gun-running, or my sister, who added wrinkles to my parents' foreheads by eloping at seventeen. Finally, though, I had to accept that no sibling had matched me in causing sleepless nights and long discussions.

For her own part, my dear, sweet mother had gone by the tragically flawed notion that "Diane knows what she's doing," while Daddy would say "*No way* she does" and judge/jury me right down off that pedestal. I was too free-spirited for his taste. In fact, in attempts to alter my course at times, Daddy gave arguments worthy of Alexander Hamilton in pompousness. I hated disappointing him, but it would have been easier to dissect my brain to please him than to follow his edicts.

Daddy never saw the swerving, switching, twitching. I'm sure if he had, there might have been empathy for my deep-fried brain. I didn't *make choices*. Roads chose me—and I just ambled along, having no earthly idea what I was supposed to be doing other than ponying up to the typewriter or computer. I kept looking for signs that I was doing the right thing, but my concentration shattered like slivers of glass every time.

Finally, I realized that one part of life that brings me glowing peace is being a nurturer: a wife, a mother, a sister, an aunt, a grandmother, a friend, a teacher. There, I feel a wellspring of happiness that just keeps on giving. Did I drown my daughter in love-sweet-love? Sure, I did, and my extreme affection for stepchildren and grandchildren also glows for anyone to see. So, fools fall in love, but we're never sorry we did.

Writer on the Ropes

Don't be surprised if you terrorize yourself. That's normal for writers. Not fun but yes, normal. I've had days when my brain flipped from one mocking clown to another until I was too exhausted to write. Funny thing is, though I have trouble finding receipts for IRS records, my brain has a well-audited file of my mistakes. In mean mode, the reel says, "I don't think you felt bad enough when you first did this, so I'm going to remind you 200 more times."

Sometimes, I feel like a little kid learning to ride a big horse. Anything I get right—and keep from falling off—is fantastic. Actually, I felt pretty good on Seaberry's back until he started trotting, the unlatched saddle turned, and I was plopped face first on the ground. This happened when I was a kid, after which I heard the adults saying, "*You have to get back on. Try again.*"

And it's the same with writing. You *never* give up. *No real writer does that.* I will never forget a magazine editor/friend who made notes for a handout to be distributed at her funeral in the car on the way to the hospital for the last time. She just had *a few more things to share.* My favorite on her list: "Floss daily. I'm dead serious." (My grandson liked that story so much that he borrowed it to use in an essay.)

Identify Your Biggest Challenge

Anyway, no matter how many "organizers" and calendars I buy, I remain—at the base of me—a disorganized individual. I have worked on this weakness, mostly in an extremely disorganized way. But if I see a magazine on the exit stand at the grocery store and a blurb promises "10 Tips for Organizing Your Kitchen," I pick it up like a robot-with-a-fetch-arm. I couldn't stop the urge if I tried.

My dream is that one of these magazine articles will be the magic elixir that changes everything. Tumbling away amid huge piles of books, papers, water bottles and appliance/car instruction manuals I've never read, I sometimes get a glimpse into why organizational ideas elude me. They don't take into account the person with stacks who just keeps thinking, "Well, if it weren't for all those things, I would have a neat house."

I'm not a hoarder, but I do have a blind spot when it comes to piles. I need to *see* stuff because things that I put in a drawer no longer exist for me. Items in bedside table drawers are forever gone missing. I need sunglasses, car keys, writing pads, birthday cards, ballpoint pens, books, and computers at arm's length or closer.

The only things that can sideline writing (for me) are live people to talk with or televised basketball games or *The Voice* and any good series. I am the recommender. If anyone wants to know the latest-greatest series, they text me. (See "The Undoing," with Nicole Kidman and Hugh Grant.) I embrace entertainment in a singular way.

Circle the Wagons

Really, the only problem with a writer's objectivity is the problem of getting stuck out there. You're like the Bubble Boy (*Seinfeld* allusion) except nicer. You're polishing a point of view. Believe in it, but also let it go occasionally and relax.

One time in Houston, I edited a book for a doctor who would reinstate every word I edited out of his 1,200-page novel that he had written on the founding of the Bayou City by the Allen brothers. Our back-and-forth became comical; I would delete 12 pages of door description, and he would "stet" it. The moral of this story is, if you hire an editor, it's not a bad idea to pay attention to parts that are marked as overblown.

As a writer, though, you *cannot* worry about critics. You can get stung by bees like a thousand times, but you do not flinch (you carry an Epi pen at all times). You are impervious; no one can kill your spirit. Even staring at a 142nd rejection letter, you are fearless; nothing can stop you. Work this right, and I promise you'll never have to eat larva in your entire life. And you definitely will get what you want from your writing—published work or simple joy or both.

Just stay engrossed by what you see as the world moves by; lap it up like the tastiest gourmet baked goods. Moving to a space outside yourself is a smart move because it erodes writers' natural tendency to be *narcissistic tools*. The more you focus on others and nature and predicaments and pleasantries, the more likely you are to avoid drugs and alcohol—and reap the best of your prancing around on earth for however many years you last.

Don't Forget People

So, what does a kid remember most when he looks back on his school days? Is it the Periodic Table or the Declaration of Independence? Is it the new school library with its well-appointed reading carrels and gorgeous wood flooring? No, the truth is, everything, even school, is about relationships, including ones you have with teachers, principals, counselors, lunchtime buddies, book characters, and coaches. A Student Wellness Report in California features one student's poignant post-COVID requiem on what she missed most during Zoom learning days: "Hugging my friends, talking to teachers, and sitting next to classmates became luxuries," said the high school freshman. "I had dreams about hugging people, and I would wake up crying." (Youth Liberty Squad).

This is your audience. Keep their humanity in mind, and you'll be a good, warm writer.

In the Long Run

Life is relatively simple. Problem is, people today work hard to make it complicated. This comes to your attention when you pass the critical age marker of fifty and begin to assess your life, your values, and your relationships. *How did I do? Was I an asset or a detriment to society?*

Ironically, when I think of things I've invested in, such as family, children, careers, and volunteer work, I can see that all of us do better when we open our hearts to that God on high who is far more important than all of the tiny human beings rattling around on the topsoil. Of course, living as Christians requires a commitment to kindness and helpfulness, which is a huge reminder that every force pulling us in a self-serving direction is a wrong signal.

Things I know for sure are these:

Watch out what you wish for when you live in a nation of enviable freedoms. Every day you choose what you want to do, where you work, how you rear your children.

Always show respect for others in every aspect of life: This includes when you talk to an AT&T rep on the phone, when you're frustrated by the salesperson who won't help you, when church leaders disappoint you.

Avoid the self-righteous Woke Mob that

declares winners and losers. These Americans have lost their sense of humor, and worse, they are an example of the loudest (not the smartest) trying to move the U.S. toward socialism. It brings to mind slogans of the fictional government of author George Orwell's dystopic *1984.* This novel is an allegory for totalitarianism, with its important lesson: *oppression is bad, and liberty is good.*

George Orwell, a Bernie Sanders-esque socialist, was interested mainly in showing that totalitarian regimes succeed only when their advocates are skilled manipulators of language. Today we see abuse-of-language on the upswing as one person brands your words "propaganda," while another protectively calls it "your truth." The reality is, we live in a time when people believe in shades of truth, shades of gender, and shades of lawlessness.

In truth, though, we are all in this together. Few of us have one iota of interest in being extremists or racists. Most of us want to support each other, find good in others, and parent in positive ways that lead to secure, happy adults. We want to salute our flag and sing "The Star-Spangled Banner." *We don't want any trouble.*

So, the answer comes in lifting people up, and that means *all people.* Tear no one and no thing down (and that includes national monuments). Keep our country free by cherishing what made this country great. Watch circumspectly what you wish for unless you're willing to bet on the Door of Unknowns over the Door of Knowns.

What will help anyone who feels discouraged by today's grim divisiveness is this: Swear allegiance to this country and stand tall for the preservation of freedoms and the continuing education of our children in U.S. history, respectful behavior, and love for all races, with no one race more important than another. There are many reasons the U.S. has survived over the years, but not one has anything to do with bashing or blame-shifting or demonizing.

Let us hope that the "American the Beautiful" movement can replace groupism and return us to a kinder and simpler America, where *all lives* matter *every day* and where children take pride in growing up in a land of dreams and optimism and harmony.

If we Americans get so intense that we forget to dance, soon we will have no reason to dance at all.

Stuck in the Middle
By Melissa Mead

My green apron had a crusty patch of syrup on the pocket, and I couldn't help but run my fingernails over it in a methodical manner—One. After. The. Other. As I was picking at the dried splatter, I couldn't help but feel as though *I* was the syrup stuck on the apron. I was stuck in a full-time barista job, and it would take something incredibly unique and special to break me out of my mold. Would I be picking at stains and smudges for the rest of my life? I was stuck in a cyclone of logging miles on my running shoes and pulling shots of espresso for minimum wage.

My fingers longed to type. At that point, I'd dabbled in some magazine writing, in fields that didn't always pique my interests. But where could I go from there? Writing a book seemed overreaching. Unfathomable really—until one day I took an order over the headset intercom for a grande nonfat chai that would change my life. This was the coffee shop where it all went down, as they say.

Each morning, the headset dug into the skin behind my ears, and there was a fun little button on the side that yielded a "walkie-talkie" function so that I could converse with the other baristas on the floor. *Confirm this. Validate that.* You know, basic things. Was that drink actually supposed to be "iced"? Were those bacon/gouda breakfast sandwiches supposed to be cooked open-faced? Does he need that cake pop cut in half? Did that lady say she wanted three ice cubes in her trenta green iced tea? I think that macchiato was supposed to be at 124 degrees and not one smidgen hotter. The headset feature was quite the little savior.

It was notable, too, that hearing folks order their food and drinks always gave me a little insight into who they could be as people, how they treated others, and perhaps what they were all about. I was always interested in learning people's stories, but I became even more attuned to hearing Diane's order, and her voice became a staple in my workday. I knew that when my ear caught wind of a grande nonfat chai in a soft Texas drawl, I would get to have a pleasant conversation that usually involved writing and my goals for the future. Most folks who came through the drive-thru window were there for one reason and one reason only. But when Diane came by, she showed interest in my writerly attributes, and it felt so refreshing to be recognized in that way.

I'll never forget the day she asked me to bring her some samples of my writing. (And that's just what I did.) I had (discreetly) been carrying a few wadded-up magazines in my front apron pocket all morning, in anticipation of being able to hand her personally my work through the window. Then the moment the magazines left my hand and passed through the vortex that separated my world and the outside world, I felt hopeful. Something was going to come of this. A published author was going to read my work and give me feedback and advice.

Now, flash forward in time, and Diane and I have collaborated on *Epic Essays* for three years, delivered it to the publisher, only to land it finally in human hands. So, who says Starbucks is a froufrou place where people go to indulge frivolous egos and frothy taste buds? I'm just saying…

Nothing ever happens unless someone reaches out. Nothing ever happens unless you write it into your story.

Bibliography

"Abraham Lincoln Quotes." Goodreads.com.
https://www.goodreads.com/author/quotes/229.Abraham_Linc
oln/. Accessed 1 June 2021.

"Ad Hominem." Wikipedia.
https://en.wikipedia.org/wiki/Ad_hominem/.

"Alice in Wonderland Quotes."
https://www.goodreads.com/work/quotes/2933712-alice-s-
adventures-in-wonderland/. Accessed 10 June 2021.

Bell-Villada, Gene H. "Themes of One Hundred Years of Solitude." 20
Jan 2004. Oprah.com. Excerpted from Gene Bell-Villada's *Garcia
Marquez: The Man and His Work*.
https://www.oprah.com/oprahsbookclub/themes-of-one-
hundred-years-of-solitude/all#ixzz720qbr97R. Accessed 10 May
2021.

"Black Arts Movement (1965-1975)." *National Archives and Records
Administration*, National Archives and Records Administration, 1
July 2020, www.archives.gov/research/african-americans/black-
power/arts/.

Blakemore, Bill. "Kubrick's Shining Secret." *Washington Post*. 12 July
1987.
https://www.washingtonpost.com/archive/lifestyle/style/1987/
07/12/kubricks-shining-secret. Accessed 1 Feb 2021.

Blume, Judy. "Are You There, God? It's Me, Margaret." 29 Apr 2014.
Atheneum Books for Young Readers.
https://judyblume.com/judy-blume-books/middle-
books/middle-margaret/.

"Britney Spears Conservatorship Timeline: Why She Has It." *Page Six*
online. 24 June 2021. `https://pagesix.com/article/britney-
spears-conservatorship-timeline-why-she-has-it/. Accessed 30
June 2021.

"Can Too Much Tech Cause ADHD Symptoms in Your Child?" 13
Aug. 2018. Cleveland Clinic.
https://health.clevelandclinic.org/can-too-much-tech-cause-
adhd-symptoms-in-your-child/.

Capote, Truman. *In Cold Blood*. 1 Feb 1994, Vintage; originally published
by Penguin in 1965 ©; excerpt reproduced with permission of
Penguin Random House LLC. ©

"Carl Sandburg Quotes." Goodreads.com.

https://www.goodreads.com/quotes/366088-shakespeare-
leonardo-da-vinci-benjamin-franklin-and-abraham-lincoln-never/.
Accessed 1 June 2021.

Carroll, Lewis. *Alice's Adventures in Wonderland/Through the Looking-Glass.*
https://www.goodreads.com/quotes/1139-she-generally-gave-
herself-very-good-advice-though-she-very/.

Chambers, Eddie. "How the Legacy of Martin Luther King, Jr. Affected
the Arts Both Then and Now." *UT News*, 15 Aug 2018.
news.utexas.edu/2018/04/04/how-the-legacy-of-martin-luther-
king-jr-affected-the-arts/.

Chbosky, Stephen. *The Perks of Being a Wallflower.*
https://www.imdb.com/title/tt1659337/.

Cisneros, Sandra. *The House on Mango Street.*
https://www.sparknotes.com/lit/mangostreet/.

Cocks, Geoffrey. "Cinema and Me: Family and History Through Film
References in Kubrick's *The Shining.*" Sense of History."
https://www.sensesofcinema.com/2020/the-shining-at-
40/family-and-history-through-film-references/.

Conroy, Pat. *The Prince of Tides.* https://patconroy.com/the-prince-of-
tides/.

Didion, Joan. *The Year of Magical Thinking.* Vintage Books, A Division of
Penguin Random House LLC: New York. 2005. © Excerpt
reproduced with permission of Penguin Random House LLC. ©

Dowd, James E. and Diane Stafford. *The Vitamin D Cure.* John Wiley &
Sons, 2012.

"Ethos Defined." Studiobinder. 27 July 2020.
https://www.studiobinder.com/blog/kairos-definition-
examples/.

"The Feminine Mystique." *Britannica.*
https://www.britannica.com/topic/The-Feminine-Mystique.

Findlen, Paula. "Propagating Propaganda." *The Public Domain Review.*
http://publicdomainreview.org/essay/propagating-propaganda/.
Creative Commons CCO.

Fitzgerald, F. Scott. *The Great Gatsby©.* excerpt from *The Great Gatsby©,*
by F. Scott Fitzgerald, reproduced with permission of The
Licensor through PLSclear©).

Fitzgerald, F. Scott. *The Great Gatsby.* `Student Edition. USA, NV, 12
July 2021. ©

Frank, Anne. *Anne Frank. The Diary of a Young Girl.*
https://www.amazon.com/Anne-Frank-Diary-Young-
Girl/dp/0553296981.

Frank, Priscilla. "A Brief History of Art Censorship From 1508 To

2014." *HuffPost*, 7 Dec. 2017. www.huffpost.com/entry/art-censorship_n_6465010/.

Friedan, Betty. "The Feminine Mystique."
    https://www.britannica.com/topic/The-Feminine-Mystique/.

Frost, Robert. "The Road Not Taken."
    https://www.poetryfoundation.org/poems/44272/the-road-not-taken

"Game of Thrones." HBO. Hulu. HBO Entertainment; co-executive producers, George R.R. Martin, Vince Gerardis, Ralph Vicinanza, Guymon Casady, Carolyn Strauss; producers, Mark Huffam, Frank Doelger; executive producers David Benioff, D.B. Weiss; created by David Benioff & D.B. Weiss; Television 360; Grok! Television; Generator Entertainment; Bighead Littlehead. Game of Thrones. The Complete First Season. New York: HBO Home Entertainment, 2012.

"Generation Z." *Wikipedia.*
    https://en.wikipedia.org/wiki/Generation_Z. Accessed 1 June 2021.

Golding, William. *The Lord of the Flies.*
    https://en.wikipedia.org/wiki/Lord_of_the_Flies.

Gordon, Mary. "The Fate of Women of Genius." *New York Times.* 12 Sep1981. https://archive.nytimes.com/www.nytimes.com/books/98/03/08/home/gordon-fate.html.

Green, John. *Looking for Alaska.*
    https://en.wikipedia.org/wiki/Looking_for_Alaska/.

Greene, Andy. "Stephen King: *The Rolling Stone* Interview." 31 Oct 2013. https://www.rollingstone.com/culture/culture-features/stephen-king-the-rolling-stone-interview-191529/.

Grose, Jessica. "Cleaning: The Final Feminist Frontier." 18 Mar 2013. *The New Republic*, posted 27 July 2021.

Handford, Martin. *Where's Waldo.* Candlewick, 25 Nov. 2019.

Henry, O. "The Gift of the Magi."
    https://en.wikipedia.org/wiki/The_Gift_of_the_Magi.

Henry, O. "The Ransom of Red Chief."
    https://en.wikipedia.org/wiki/The_Ransom_of_Red_Chief/.

Hemingway, Ernest. *The Old Man and the Sea.* Scribner, 1952.

Hillenbrand, Laura. *Unbroken.* New York: Random House, 2010.

Hinton, S.E. *The Outsiders.* Viking Books for Young Readers, Platinum Edition. 10 Apr 2006.Excerpts from THE OUTSIDERS by S.E. Hinton, copyright © 1967, renewed 1995 by S.E. Hinton. Used by permission of Viking Children's Books, an imprint of Penguin Young Readers Group, a division of Penguin Random House

LLC. All rights reserved.

Hochschild, Arlie. *The Second Shift: Working Families and The Revolution at Home*. Penguin Books, Revised Edition. 31 Jan 2012.

"How to Be a Good Wife (1950s Style)." Dr. Nancy website. Posted 9 Aug. 2010. https://www.drnancyoreilly.com/how-to-be-a-good-wife-1950s-style/.

Jones, Carolyn. *EdSource* online. 13 May 2020. https://edsource.org/2020/student-anxiety-depression-increasing-during-school-closures-survey-finds/631224.

Jones, Susan. "The Truth about Why Women Still Can't Have It All." 2012. https://www.americanbar.org/groups/litigation/committees/woman-advocate/practice/2012/truth-why-women-still-cant-have-it-all/.

"Kairos Definition and Meaning: Kairos Rhetoric Explained." Video. Studiobinder.com. 27 July 2020. https://www.studiobinder.com/blog/kairos-definition-examples/.

King, Martin L. "Letter from the Birmingham Jail." San Francisco: Harper San Francisco, 1994. Print.

King, Stephen. *The Shining* (paperback). Anchor Books. A Division of Random House. New York. 2013. Originally published by Doubleday. 1977.

Knowles, John. *A Separate Peace*. Scribner: New York. 1959.

Kubrick, Stanley, Stephen King, and Diane Johnson. *The Shining*. Warner Bros. Pictures, 1980.

Lee, Harper. *To Kill a Mockingbird*. Harper Perennial Modern Classics. *2002. ©1960. Renewed 1988.*

"Letter from Birmingham Jail," copyright: © 1963 Dr. Martin Luther King, Jr. © renewed 1991 Coretta Scott King.

Llorente, Renzo. "Neil Postman." *Encyclopedia Britannica*, 4 Mar. 2021, https://www.britannica.com/biography/Neil-Postman. Accessed 4 Aug. 2021.

Lockhart, E. *We Were Liars*. *https://en.wikipedia.org/wiki/We_Were_Liars/*.

London, Jack. *The Call of the Wild*. Sterling Publishing, 2005.

Mapes, Julian. "Lady Gaga Explains the Meat Dress: 'It's No Disrespect.'" *Billboard*. 13 Sept 2010. https://www.billboard.com/articles/news/956399/lady-gaga-explains-her-meat-dress-its-no-disrespect/.

"Mariachi." *Britannica*. *https://www.britannica.com/art/mariachi*.

Mariachi Plaza Directory and Service Center. "Mariachi."

http://mariachiplazalosangeles.com/site/.

"Mariachi." Wikipedia. https://en.wikipedia.org/wiki/Mariachi/.

Marquez, Gabriel Garcia. *One Hundred Years of Solitude*. Harper & Row. 1970. HarperCollins Publishers. Originally published in Argentina in 1967 by Editorial Sudamericanos, S.A. Buenos Aires, under the title *Cien Anos de Soledad*.

McKenzie, Steven. "*The Shining* Theories Explored in Spooky New Dcoumentary."23 Oct 2002. Accessed 14 Nov. 2020. Mencken, Henry L. "The Penalty of Death." https://www.lmtsd.org/cms/lib/PA01000427/Centricity/Domai n/231/Death%20Penalty%20essays.pdf/.

Michaels, Stephen. "American Freedom: Sinclair Lewis and the Open Road." *The Public Domain Review.* https://publicdomainreview.org/essay/american-freedom-sinclair-lewis-and-the-open-road/. Creative Commons CCO.

Milbrandt, Melody K. "Understanding the Role of Art in Social Movements and Transformation." *Journal of Art for Life*, 15 Mar 2010, journals.flvc.org/jafl/article/view/84087/.

"MLA Formatting and Style Guide." *The Purdue OWL*, 2 Aug. 2016, owl.english.purdue.edu/owl/resource/747/01/. Accessed 2 April 2020.

Morrison, Toni. Song of Solomon. https://www.sparknotes.com/lit/solomon/.

Newport Beach Public Library Online Databases. Newport Beach, California.

O'Brien, Tim. *The Things They Carried*. https://en.wikipedia.org/wiki/The_Things_They_Carried/.

Old Navy ad video. https://www.youtube.com/watch?v=PKWisayP0V8/. Accessed 10 June 2021.

Palacio, R.J., *Wonder.* Knopf, 2012.

Peacock, Tim. *U Discover Music.* 15 August 2020. "Best Woodstock Performances: 15 Acts That Defined the Festival" https://www.udiscovermusic.com/stories/best-woodstock-performances/.

Poe, Edgar Allan. "Annabelle Lee." https://www.poetryfoundation.org/poems/44885/annabel-lee/.

Poe, Edgar Allan. "The Raven." https://thisamericanlyric2015.qwriting.qc.cuny.edu/files/2015/0 1/Poe-The-Raven.pdf/.

Poe, Edgar Allan. "The Tell-Tale Heart." https://americanenglish.state.gov/files/ac/resource_files/the_tel

l-tale_heart_0.pdf/.

"Poetry of the Black Arts Movement: Overview." *Research Guides*, 1 July 2019. libguides.wustl.edu/poetry-bam/overview.

Purdue Online Writing Lab. https://owl.purdue.edu/. Accessed 1 June 2021.

"Remembering An 'Unbroken' Hero Of WWII." *Weekend Edition Saturday*, 5 July 2014. Gale Literature Resource Center, https://link.gale.com/apps/doc/A374339179/LitRC. Accessed 14 Nov 2020.

"Rhetoric." Aristotle. Borrowed from Supersummary.com. https://www.supersummary.com/rhetoric/summary/.

Rottenberg, Catherine. *"The Rise of Neoliberal Feminism.* Oxford University Press." Article in Cultural Studies, vol. 28, 2014, issue 3. https://www.tandfonline.com/doi/abs/10.1080/09502386.2013.857361/. Reproduced through permission of the Licensor through PLSclear.

Rowling, J.K. *Harry Potter and the Goblet of Fire*. Published by Arthur A. Levine Books, an imprint of Scholastic, Inc., July 2000.

Schaffer, Sarah. "Dining Well on Woolf." 18 Oct 1996. https://www.thecrimson.com/article/1996/10/18/dining-well-on-woolf-pione-cannot/Shakespeare, William. *Hamlet*. Updated Edition. Folger Shakespeare Library. 1992, 2012. Simon & Schuster.

Slaughter, Anne-Marie. "Why Women Still Can't Have It All." *The Atlantic*. July/Aug 2012. https://www.theatlantic.com/magazine/archive/2012/07/why-women-still-cant-have-it all/309020/.

Spiller, Roger. "The Real War." *American Heritage*. Nov 1989. https://www.americanheritage.com/real-war/.

Stockton. Frank. *"The Lady, or the Tiger." Wikipedia.* https://en.wikipedia.org/wiki/The_Lady,_or_the_Tiger%3F.

Studiobinder. "Kairos: Definition." https://www.studiobinder.com/blog/kairos-definition-examples/.

Swift, Jonathon. *A Modest Proposal.* https://www.gutenberg.org/files/1080/1080-h/1080-h.htm/. "Syllogisms." Supersummary.com/syllogism/.

Thiele, Rebecca. "Symbolism of the Holocaust in the horror movie *The Shining*/WMUK." 15 Nov. 2012. *BBC World Service.* https://www.wmuk.org/post/room-237-symbolism-holocaust-horror-movie-shining#stream/https://www.bbc.com/news/uk-scotland-highlands-islands-19789783/.

"Top Thirty Quotes of Simon Cowell." Simon Cowell.
https://www.inspiringquotes.us/author/9650-simon-cowell/).

Twain, Mark. *Adventures of Huckleberry Finn*. Barnes & Noble Classics,
2003. First published in the UK in 1884, and in the U.S. in 1885.

Twain, Mark. *The Adventures of Tom Sawyer*. Puffin Classics, 1950. First
published in 1876.

"Understanding the Nuances of ADHD with Dr. Michael Mano." 13
Feb 2019. Cleveland Clinic website.
https://my.clevelandclinic.org/podcasts/health-
essentials/understanding-the-nuances-of-adhd-with-dr-michael-
manos/.

Waycott, Laurel. "Propagating Propaganda." 17 Mar 2021. *The Public
Domain Review*.
https://publicdomainreview.org/essay/propagating-
propaganda/. Creative Commons CCO. Accessed 1 Aug. 2021.

West, Nathaneal. *The Day of the Locust*. SparkNotes Editors. "The Day of
the Locust." *SparkNotes.com*. Sparknotes, LLC. 2005. URL.

Westerfeld, Scott. *Uglies*. 3 May 2011. Simon & Schuster Books for
Young Readers, Reissue Edition.

Wilde, Oscar. *The Picture of Dorian Gray*.
https://www.gutenberg.org/files/174/174-h/174-h.htm.
Accessed 10 Oct 2021.

Wilson, Sonia. "I Am My Own Heroine." 2 Sep 2020. *The Public Domain
Review*. https://publicdomainreview.org/essay/I-am-my-own-
heroine/. Creative Commons CCO.

Wood, Bryan. "The Social Influence of Good vs. Evil." *HuffPost*. 6 Dec.
2017. https://www.huffpost.com/entry/good-vs-
evil_b_2831488?guccounter=1&guce_referrer/. Accessed 1 June
2021.

Youth Liberty Squad. California Student Wellness Survey Summary.
Sept. 2020. https://www.schoolcounselor-
ca.org/Files/Student%20Wellness%20Survey%20Summary%205
-08-20.pdf/. Accessed 1 June 2021.

Zusak, Markus. *The Book Thief. Reprint edition*. 11 Sept 2007. Knopf
Books for Young Readers. https://www.amazon.com/Book-
Thief-Marku Zusak/.

Meet the Authors

Your Life Is About to Change!

You can learn to write like a pro! Bestselling author/tutor **Diane Stafford**, after years of seeing teens struggle with essays, joined English teacher/writer Melissa Mead to write *Epic Essays in 30 Minutes: Easy Tips for Writing A+ Essays* as a handy guide for middle school and high school writers. Follow their process, and become the star writer you want to be. (A summa cum laude college grad, Stafford has a degree in English, lives and tutors in Newport Beach, California, and has 14 published books.)

Teacher/tutor Melissa Mead has taught in three school districts in Federal Way, Washington; Newport Beach, California; San Antonio, Texas. Now she teaches English at John Wood Middle School in San Antonio. An elite runner who got her masters at the University of California, Irvine, she was a Starbucks barista when she met Diane Stafford, and they began writing *Epic Essays in 30 Minutes*. This book is for *you*!

Acknowledgments

Melissa and I want to thank the many students we have taught and tutored. We learned from them as they learned from us, and we happily shared our love for reading and writing. Also, we appreciate having parents who read to us and modeled writing stories, letters, lists, and thank-you notes. Both of us are grateful, too, for friends and family members who encouraged us to keep working on *Epic Essays* and told us that they believed young people could benefit from the book.

A special thank you to Patrick Graber, who was our diligent reader and pointed out places where the book needed tightening up. Special supporters in getting this book to the publisher were my daughter Jennifer and my stepchildren Matt, Laura, Molly, Patrick, and Cita, as well as 18 grandchildren who helped make this book a reality by serving as models and guinea pigs. In particular, we thank our designer, Cita Graber. We couldn't have made it to the finish line without her talent, patience, and diligence. Kudos to Greg Graber for proofreading and editing.

We also thank the book and article authors mentioned and quoted in *Epic Essays* because, as all teachers know, examples are vital to the learning process. The excerpts from excellent books and articles make this book a teaching tool that we hope will entertain and inform. Melissa and I are donating 10 percent of profits to buy the books excerpted in *Epic Essays* for teens who lack access to great books. We're excited about the "pass it on" concept that got us from our Starbucks meetup to today, when we joyfully publish a book that shares insights, ideas, and, hopefully, excitement about reading and writing.

On a personal note, I whisper heavenward thanks to my wonderful and brilliant husband, Greg Munoz, the love of my life, who died two months before this book was published. Greg was proud of my writing, and I will forever be proud of him for being the best imaginable judge, father, friend, husband, colleague, and brother. Truly, nothing I do will ever be the same without my brown-eyed handsome man beside me.

"They are not long, the days of wine and roses:

Out of a misty dream

Our path emerges for a while, then closes

Within a dream"

—Ernest Dowson

Made in the USA
Columbia, SC
29 November 2021

49852854R00215